Mark(s) of the Beast

It's More Than Just a Number

D1518184

HISROAD PUBLISHING

HISROAD PUBLISHING

Mark(s) of the Beast: It's More Than Just a Number

Copyright © 2019 by Martin W Sondermann

Hisroad Publishing, Boise, Idaho 83704

ISBN 9781095405376 (Print Version Only)

Printed in USA by Hisroad Publishing, Boise, Idaho

Table of Contents

Dedication

To my mom....

She inspired me and encouraged me to serve our King!

Preface

Whenever a new book is published in the Christian community relating to eschatology, prophecy, end-times events, or the Book of Revelation I am cautious—and you should be too. After all, there are many winds of doctrine that tend to sweep through the believer's landscape like a wildfire following multiple seasons of drought and deficiency. This fact seems especially true these days in the era of instant communication multiplied by the massive web of social media and self-published works that crowd the precious paths of time and energy. To quote Charles Dickens in his classic work A Tale of Two Cities[i],

> It was the best of times, it was the worst of times, it was the age of wisdom, it was the age of foolishness, it was the epoch of belief, it was the epoch of incredulity, it was the season of light, it was the season of darkness, it was the spring of hope, it was the winter of despair, we had everything before us, we had nothing before us, we were all going direct to Heaven, we were all going direct the other way—in short, the period was so far like the present period, that some of its noisiest authorities insisted on its being received, for good or for evil, in the superlative degree of comparison only.

Martin W Sondermann

This current epoch, in which we find ourselves, has brought with it exponential growth in nearly every area of science, technology, and information. This can be an overwhelming stream of abundance that causes many of us to stay close to the shoreline so as not to drown. With this ocean of increase, both the powers of light, and of darkness, have been given a massive number of tools to do the work of the kingdom in which they serve. This modern age has certainly brought with it an overload of information filled with pitfalls, false doctrines, vain imaginations and the like, yet, it has also brought with it a tremendous amount of knowledge and study material for the Body of Christ. As Bible believing Christians we should not be surprised at this growth. After all, the Scriptures told us as much in Daniel chapter 12 verse 4, *"But as for you, Daniel, conceal these words and seal up the book until the end of time; many will go back and forth, and knowledge will increase." (NASB)[ii]*

Introduction

Before diving into the topic of this book I want to give the reader a word of caution. I also want those reading to understand the heart of this work, and the encouragement I send your way. First, do not blindly trust or accept the opinions, thoughts, and understanding of doctrine, theology, or eschatology presented within these pages, or within any pages outside of the Holy Scriptures. What I want to challenge each individual to do is to simply do what the Scripture states in 1 Thessalonians chapter 5 verse 21, *"Prove all things; hold fast that which is good" (KJV)*[iii] The Bible also instructs us in 2 Timothy 2:15 to, *"Study to show thyself approved unto God, a workman that needeth not to be ashamed, rightly dividing the Word of Truth." (KJV)* This is the standard that all believers should follow, and I for one will not be offended if you think I have fallen off my proverbial rocker. I simply ask that you let me know where you believe I have erred— according to the Scriptures. Also, please know this book is not being written to be different, take a contrary view for contrary's sake, argue, or try to prove to you I have some kind of superior intelligence or secret knowledge. This book comes from the heart of someone who loves to study God's Word, and very much enjoys sharing what he learns with believers and non-believers alike.

Chapter 1

The Focus

The Evil Number

The "Mark of the Beast" is a phrase most Christians and many non-Christians are familiar with. It is a term heavily packed with meaning, and often decorated by a gaudy amount of tradition, belief, and superstition. You can also be sure that in most cases whenever this term is mentioned it is usually followed by a reference to the number 6-6-6. After all, everyone knows that 666 is the mark of the beast. I mean, everyone knows that this particular number is downright evil. Don't they?

Within the pages of this work I will attempt to make a case that this scary evil number "666" is actually not the mark of the beast, or rather, it is <u>not the only</u> mark of the beast. While that may not sound valid to you right now, or even valuable, I believe it to be both. With a close examination of the Holy Bible I am going to attempt to prove to you that this number is only one facet of the coming mark that many will receive in their right hands or foreheads as a way to align themselves with the coming one-world government, its religion, its economy, and its diabolical leader. I will also look at some hints in the Scriptures that seem to indicate different types or classes of people, and how that will actually determine which of the mark they receive.

Taking a Step Back

Since this topic is drawn from the waters of the Book of Revelation, I feel it's necessary to first take a step back and explain that I whole-heartily believe that no single verse of the Bible should be interpreted without context. Each verse in the Bible is after all, eternally connected with every other word, verse, chapter and book of the Holy Scriptures. In saying that I also want the reader to understand that whenever I teach through the Book of Revelation itself, or any part, portion, or passage of it, I make sure those hearing the teaching understand what this amazing book is all about. To do this I first start with what this book is NOT about. It is not about the Apostle John, although the Holy Spirit inspired him to pen this book while imprisoned on the island of Patmos. It's also not about the Anti-Christ, his earthly reign, and all the strange and crazy things that go along with it. It's certainly not about a single denomination or pseudo-Christian cult despite what some claim while trying to massage, bend, and manipulate the words of Revelation to form an image of what they might desire. No friends, this is not a book about any religion, it's not about Lucifer, it's not about world governments, it's not about false religion, it's not about strange signs, it's not about this world's destruction, and it's certainly not about the mark of the beast. This book is about one thing and one thing only. Or, a better description would be that this book is simply about one person, and one person alone. It's ALL about our Great God and King, Jesus Christ!

The Outline

The Book of Revelation is the Revelation of Jesus Christ, and with all due respect to the Apostle John it is not "The Revelation of St. John the Divine." This book is not about anything or anyone except Jesus.

The name of the book, "Revelation" is derived from the Greek word "Apokalupsis" from where we get our English word apocalypse. However, that word (apocalypse) has received a lot of bad press over the centuries, and it has become synonymous with devastation, and the final war that the world will endure. Although most people don't realize that final war will not even really happen. It's interrupted by King Jesus. But, that's another study for another day. For today's study, the true meaning of the word Revelation or Apokalupsis, is to "reveal, to disclose, or to unveil". It is an unveiling! The question then becomes what is being unveiled?

In chapter 1 verse 19 of Revelation the Lord gives us the outline of the entire book. *"Therefore, write the things which you have seen, and the things which are, and the things which will take place after these things."(NASB)*

Here the Lord sends a message to John giving him the entire breakdown of the Book of Revelation in one sentence. This was just after John had an encounter with a messenger that showed him something breathtaking and mind blowing. John was given the ability to see Jesus, the Living God, the resurrected King of Kings and Lord of Lords, Yeshua Hamashiach, Jesus the Messiah. He had just witnessed our Lord in His glorious resurrected form. The verses in chapter 1 leading up to verse 19 give us an amazing picture of who Jesus is, and through the power of the Holy Spirit John was able to describe it to us in a way that has so much depth and power.

Mark(s) of the Beast

We also know the messenger of Revelation instructs John to pen seven letters to seven churches in chapters 2-3, and then to communicate future events in chapters 4 through 22. These three sections are the outline of the Book of Revelation.

Seven Churches

A quick side-note about these letters to the seven churches; I believe it is important for us to understand that these seven letters were indeed written to seven churches during John's day. In fact, they were seven churches that John himself had been a pastor to in Asia Minor (modern day Turkey). But as God does many times in His Holy Scriptures, He makes these letters relevant for all of us. These seven letters aren't just for the churches in John's day, but they stand as examples for the Church (the Body of Christ) throughout history. This of course, includes all of us alive in the modern age. The issues and topics addressed in those letters are relevant in any time during the Church age. Thus, *"the things which are."*

But before we move on, I also believe those letters move into the realm of the prophetic. I encourage everyone to study this out when you have some time. I believe these seven amazing letters packed with so much instruction and

Martin W Sondermann

correction, also carry with them a prophetic timeline for those who have eyes to see. If you study it out, I believe you will come to the same conclusion that I did. If you examine each letter according to a historical timeline you will see that there is a remarkable aligning of each letter with a stage of Church history. I also believe we are currently living in the days of Laodicea. But, again, that is a study for another day.

After These Things

Lastly, the outline in verse 19 of Revelation chapter 1 covers, *"The things which will take place after these things."* The question then, is what is meant by "after these things"? I believe it's speaking of the first two things in the outline. After the appearance to John of the glorified resurrected Christ, and after the Church age. I sincerely believe this passage refers to the fact that Jesus is giving John a divine order of things. In a paraphrased summary I believe this is what Jesus has instructed John to do; He tells him to write what you have just seen, and then write about the things which currently are, and then write about future events.

Also, it must be noted that many Bible teachers, scholars and Pastors point to the phrase *"after these things"* in the Greek language as something significant. I'm personally not a Greek scholar, but I trust those that are. From my study of this I have found that this phrase *"after these things"*, is *"meta tauta"* in the Greek language. This is important because there seems to be a clear transition in Revelation chapter 4 verse 1, *"__After these things__ I looked, and behold, a door standing open in heaven, and the first voice which I had heard, like the sound of a trumpet speaking with me, said, "Come up here, and I will show you what must take place after these things."(NASB)*

That familiar phrase *"after these things"*, or "meta tauta" begins verse 1 of chapter 4, and I believe it signals a transition of current events (the Church) to future events. I believe we also see a picture of the Rapture of the Church in that same verse when a door opens in Heaven, and John is taken up by the command of a voice like a trumpet. This appears to happen at the beginning of the tribulation, and not in the middle or at the end. Of course, you are welcome to disagree. I know there are several opinions about the timing of the Rapture of the Church, and all I ask is that you don't stop reading this study just because we don't agree on this particular issue. After all, it is a future event, and we won't know for sure who interpreted Scripture properly until it actually happens.

Future Events

From chapter 4 through chapter 22 in Revelation we are then dealing with future events. That is, except for a brief review in chapter 12 when the Lord seems to give a historical overview of the story of the Jewish nation, and the arrival of our Lord in human flesh. Of course, like many other things in this book, that is also up for debate. We will look at this closer in another chapter.

The Summary of the Book

So, putting it all together we see the clear outline of the Book of Revelation (the Unveiling). In chapter 1 verse 19 the outline of Revelation is broken down into three categories. 1. Write the things which you have seen; the glorified resurrected Christ. 2. Write the things which are; Church history. 3. Write the things which will take place after these things, which is referring to future events. A closer look reveals that each of those categories is centered on Jesus. As I said, this book is all about Him, and should be studied as such. It's an "unveiling" of His Person, His People, and His Plan.

1. His Person: Chapter 1 (Glorified Christ)

Mark(s) of the Beast

2. His People: Chapters 2-3 (The Church)

3. His Plan: Chapters 4-22 (Future Events)

Those "future events" can be further broken down with chapters 4 and 5 showing us the amazing and wonderful honeymoon of the Church with Jesus in Heaven. Chapters 6 to 19 I believe then give us an insight into the tribulation period which will overtake the earth. This "tribulation" will be a time in which God will pour out His wrath on a world that has rejected His Son Jesus. It will also be a time in which God will deal with Israel corporately in a response to His promised 70th week written about in the book of Daniel. But you guessed it, that's another study for another day.

Lastly Chapters 20-22 of Revelation deal with the second coming of Christ, the setting up of His Millennial Kingdom, binding Satan for a 1000-year-period, releasing the devil for a short period of time, the great white throne judgment, sealing the fate of Lucifer as he is thrown into the lake of fire along with the Anti-Christ and False Prophet, and finally the creation of a new Heaven and a new earth where believers will dwell with God forever, and ever! Amen!

It's All About Him!

Martin W Sondermann

It doesn't matter if you are talking about the seven seals, the seven trumpets, or the seven bowls. It doesn't matter if you are speaking of Satan's deception, the anti-Christ, the false prophet, Babylon, or the Harlot, all of this, and everything else in Revelation is contained within the plan of Jesus. If you study this book (Revelation) or anything in it, and you miss the focus on Jesus, then I tell you that you have missed the entire meaning of the book.

This is my encouragement to you as we go forward to study a portion of the Book of Revelation. Please keep in mind that even the mark of the beast is something that God will allow to divide those that are His from those that have rejected Him. After all, nothing has, or ever will happen, that the Lord didn't already know about and allow so that His Kingdom and His will would be accomplished.

Chapter 2

Context, Context, Context

Get 20/20 Vision

To understand the topic of the "Mark of the Beast," we must first get some context. I once heard a Pastor teach that if you are looking at a particular passage of Scripture you should always get 20/20 vision. What he meant by this was that you should, at the very least, look at the 20 verses prior to the passage you're studying, and the 20 verses after. This sounded like solid advice at the time, and it has served me well over the years in my own personal study of Scripture.

The main passage we will be studying for the purposes of this book is found in Revelation chapter 13 verses 16-18. It reads as follows; *"16 And he causeth all, both small and great, rich and poor, free and bond, to receive a mark in their right hand, or in their foreheads: 17 And that no man might buy or sell, save he that had the mark, or the name of the beast, or the number of his name. 18 Here is wisdom. Let him that hath understanding count the number of the beast: for it is the number of a man; and his number is Six hundred threescore and six." (KJV)*

First thing we must note is that the number found in verse 18 has become synonymous with evil. *"Six hundred threescore and six,"* or 6-6-6 is found all over popular culture in books, movies, television, and even in everyday conversations. Most people, especially in western culture, have heard some kind of reference to 666, and many have opinions about the number and its relationship to evil.

The Devil's Cheeseburger

I remember one time at a fast food restaurant I was giving my order to a very interesting young man. After all, I love a good cheeseburger, and I was famished. The young man taking my order was tattooed and pierced, and his hair was died a very different color of blue in the front and shaved on the sides. He was sharing some very colorful language with his co-workers before stopping to take my order. He rang up my items, and on the screen the total came up as $6.66. Well, I didn't care for the total, I will be honest, but I simply handed him my debit card.

"Oh man," he said in an elevated voice, "You don't want that total man."

Mark(s) of the Beast

"I don't mind," I stated, because I was tired and very hungry, and wasn't willing at that point to dive into the conversation.

"No way man, that's the number of the Devil. That's not a cool number," he added.

I stopped for a second, and realized this could be a good way to witness to him so I asked, "So are you a Christian then?"

"No, I wouldn't say that, but my mom is, but everyone knows that number is bad news."

I couldn't believe the opening. I looked at him and said, "Ya, I know people think that number is bad news, but to me it's just a number. And, I already have the good news, so the bad news doesn't scare me."

The young server laughed strangely, went silent for a moment, but then as the wheels in his mind seemed to come to a screeching halt he blurted out, "How is that good news? I don't understand what you mean by that."

I went on to tell him that the number itself wasn't the good news, and I shared the real good news with him in the form of the Gospel. I explained to him that every human

Martin W Sondermann

being is in a fallen condition, and have a disease called sin, that we are born that way. I also explained the Cross, and how Jesus has given us a remedy for our condition, and what that means for mankind. Now, as much as I would like to tell you he came to Christ that day—he didn't. But it was a nice conversation, and while he wasn't "against Jesus," his words not mine; he could not see his need to receive what Christ did for him on the Cross nearly two-thousand years ago. He was simply blind to the facts, and yet he knew about the number 6-6-6.

Leaving that restaurant, I started to think about how the world knows all about the number 6-6-6, and how almost everyone who knows about it, equates it with evil. It made me start to ponder if that number is so recognizable then how will any person during the tribulation take a number if it's so blatant and obvious? It caused me to go back to the Scriptures and study the topic like never before. As I did, I found some amazing things about the passage relating to the mark of the beast, and it made me realize that the world has been conditioned to think one thing about the mark, but the Scriptures didn't exactly teach it the same way.

Mark(s) of the Beast

Back to Our Glasses

Now, before we dive into what the passage says in relation to 6-6-6 and the mark of the beast let's get some clarity. Using the 20/20 model of studying let's look at the 20 verses that follow this passage in Revelation 13. Those verses just happen to be all of chapter 14, which contains 20 verses.

Looking at those 20 verses that follow the passage we will be focusing on in this book, we see that there is much value, and many amazing things that can deepen our understanding of the book of Revelation. We see 144,000 Jewish men selected from 12 tribes of Israel singing a song only they can learn. We also notice that not every tribe of Israel is represented in that group. In fact, two different names of tribes are left out, and one of those tribes is completely absent from participation. This is a huge study within its self, and I encourage everyone to study it out. For the sake of this study today, there is not a lot in chapter 14 that brings a clearer vision or understanding to the mark of the beast at this point. We will come back to the 144,000 in a later chapter. So, with that in mind, we will move to the 20 verses leading up to our central passage.

Martin W Sondermann

Twenty Verses Prior: Revelation 12:13-13:15

The 20 verses prior to Revelation chapter 13 verses 16-18 start in Chapter 12 at verse 13 and continue to chapter 13 verse 15. Revelation 12 verses 13-17 read as follows; *"13 And when <u>the dragon</u> saw that he was cast unto the earth, he persecuted <u>the woman</u> which brought forth the <u>man child</u>. 14 And to the woman were given two wings of a great eagle, that she might fly into the wilderness, into her place, where she is nourished for a time, and times, and half a time, from the face of the serpent 15 And the serpent cast out of his mouth water as a flood after the woman, that he might cause her to be carried away of the flood. 16 And the earth helped the woman, and the earth opened her mouth, and swallowed up the flood which the dragon cast out of his mouth. 17 And the dragon was wroth with the woman and went to make war with the remnant of her seed, which keep the commandments of God, and have the testimony of Jesus Christ." (KJV)*

In this last part of chapter 12 we see that the dragon, who is Satan, when seeing that he had been cast to earth persecuted the "woman" that brought forth the "man child." If you study this out, I believe you will see a clear connection to the "woman" in this chapter with Israel and the "man child" being Jesus Christ Himself. However, to see this we must jump back a little further in our 20/20 method, but only a few verses.

Israel and Jesus

Revelation chapter 12 verse 1 speaks of this mysterious woman; *"And there appeared a great wonder in heaven; a woman clothed with the sun, and the moon under her feet, and upon her head a crown of twelve stars:" (KJV)*

I believe when studying the Bible, we should always look to Scripture as the primary source of interpreting Scripture. In other words, we should use the proper hermeneutic allowing Scripture to interpret Scripture. Therefore, we look for other passages that relate to the passage we are studying for context, clues and connections. In using this method searching the Word of God we do see another time where the imagery of the sun, the moon, and stars make an appearance. This was the dream of Joseph in Genesis 37 in which he sees his mother, father, and brothers as the sun, the moon, and eleven stars. Genesis 37 verse 9 reads; *"And he dreamed yet another dream, and told it his brethren, and said, Behold, I have dreamed a dream more; and, behold, the sun and the moon and the eleven stars made obeisance to me." (KJV)*

"But Wait!" You might say. Revelation says twelve stars, but Genesis says eleven stars so what is the deal here pal?

Well, I am so glad you asked. You are so smart, and your questions are outstanding! I mean seriously, amazing questions.

I believe the proper interpretation of this difference can be easily explained. You see this is Joseph's dream. Who is Joseph? He is one of the sons of Jacob, also known as Israel. In this passage, since Joseph is the one having the dream, and a brother to the other men who are pictured as eleven stars, I believe he is the twelfth star. And, because his father is Jacob, who later became Israel, and because the twelve tribes of Israel derive from these twelve brothers, this appears to be the way to understand the Revelation chapter 12 passage. This woman appears to be a picture of Israel.

I think we can also understand this woman represents Israel when we see Satan's reaction to her. After all, we know from history that Satan has had a hand in persecution of the Jewish people. One of the biggest reasons is the fact that God used the Jewish people to bring forth our Messiah. I also contend that God made an unbreakable covenant with the nation of Israel through Abraham (Genesis 15), and if somehow Satan could wipe out the Jewish people from the face of the planet, he could make God a liar, and in doing so defeat Him. But we as believers know this is impossible even if Satan is so delusional as to think it would be. Just as a side note, for those who believe God is somehow done with Israel, I would suggest you study out Romans 11. Also, you must study the fact that the "Abrahamic Covenant," and the "Mosaic Covenant," are two different things.

Now, the reason I believe that the "man child" in Chapter 12 is speaking of Jesus is a bit more cut-and-dry. This is because verse 4 of this same chapter tells us that this "man child" is future King of the world and has a throne in Heaven. Verse 4 reads; *"And she brought forth a man child, who was to rule all nations with a rod of iron: and her child was caught up unto God, and to his throne." (KJV)*

Martin W Sondermann

I think if you look at this verse it's pretty clear that this man child is going to *"rule all nations with a rod of iron"*, and He also has His own *"throne"*. It seems like a clear description of our Lord.

More evidence to support the historical account theory of the first five verses of Revelation 12 is that we also see that Satan tried to kill Jesus once he was born (Verse 4). We know this attempt to kill Jesus as a young child was done through the actions of Herod, but certainly influenced by Satan. We also know the rest of the story. We know that Jesus overcame Satan, died on the Cross for our sins, rose again from the dead, and then ascended into Heaven where He went to prepare a place for His precious bride. And, I believe it is the ascension pictured in verse 5; *"was caught up unto God, and to his throne"*.

We also receive background relating to the fall of Satan in this section, and what his actions caused. In verse 4 it states; *"And his tail drew the third part of the stars of heaven, and did cast them to the earth:"* I believe this is referring to the fact that when Satan rebelled, he took a third of the angels of heaven with him.

Mark(s) of the Beast

When you look at the entire passage in Revelation 12 it appears as if early in the chapter God is giving us a quick review of the historical account of the Jewish nation, the first coming of Jesus Christ, and the fall and murderous actions of Satan. He then transitions to future events that will occur during the tribulation in a way that shows us the continuation of the battle. I believe this was a way for the Holy Spirit to give the reader of Revelation context of what will be happening during the tribulation, who it will impact, and what the plans of Satan will be. But, not only that, it also reminds us that Jesus is on the Throne, and in complete control. After all, we see later in the Chapter that Satan is further cast down out of heaven by Jesus (Verse 9). I believe this will be done so that Jesus can enjoy his honeymoon with His Bride, and to remove "the accuser of the brethren" from the party!

More Persecution to Come

After this background information we then jump back into the time of the tribulation period. In verse 6 we see *"the woman"* or Israel, fleeing into the wilderness for three and a half years where God will keep the faithful remnant safe. In my opinion this will be the brutal persecution of the

Jewish people during the tribulation, especially those who come to faith in Yeshua. Many of the Jews will be killed during that time, but God will save a faithful remnant, and hide them for three-and-a-half-years. Many scholars believe it will be a place called Petra in the country of Jordan. But, that's another study for another day. (You are going to get sick of this expression, if you haven't already).

Moving into Revelation Chapter 13

As we move into Chapter 13 of Revelation, we can build upon what we have learned so far by looking at how this evil worldly kingdom of Satan is going to be built, and how Satan will raise up his own kind of messiah. Revelation chapter 13 starting at verse 1, *"And I stood upon the sand of the sea, and saw a beast rise up out of the sea, having seven heads and ten horns, and upon his horns ten crowns, and upon his heads the name of blasphemy. (KJV)*

John sees a beast rise up out of the sea. Understand that many times in the Bible *"the sea"* can refer in symbolic form as gentile nations. I know that seems a bit strange, but study it out. John sees this beast rising from *"the sea"* or gentile nations, (gentile nations are any nation that is not

Mark(s) of the Beast

Israel). It has *"seven heads and ten horns, and upon his horns ten crowns."* We pause there to build the foundation of context.

Seven Heads

The first thing I want to address is the *"seven heads"*. The Scripture tells us in Revelation 17 verse 9 that these *"seven heads"* are seven mountains. *"And here is the mind which hath wisdom. The seven heads are <u>seven mountains</u>, on which the woman sitteth. (KJV)*

Some scholars try to equate the *"seven mountains"* with the seven hills that Rome sits on physically, but I think when we look closer at Scripture it doesn't say that. God is very specific, and so why would he call hills mountains, or vice versa? Now, I don't base my entire argument on this, but if God wanted to say hills, I believe He would have said hills. However, I do believe there is a connection to a revived Roman Empire and the coming Anti-Christ kingdom, I just don't think the seven mountains in this verse are speaking about the city of Rome itself. Instead, I believe the Roman Empire is part of what being described here, and that is simply, seven kingdoms. Many times, the word "mountain" or "mountains" in the

Martin W Sondermann

Scriptures refers to kingdoms. Examples; The Bible calls the Babylonian Kingdom a *"destroying mountain"* in Jeremiah 51 verses 24-25. An even a greater example of this understanding can be found relating to the Kingdom of our Lord Jesus. Isaiah 2:2-3 states, *"And it shall come to pass in the last days, that the mountain of the LORD'S house shall be established in the top of the mountains and shall be exalted above the hills; and all nations shall flow unto it. 3 And many people shall go and say, Come ye, and let us go up to the mountain of the LORD, to the house of the God of Jacob; and he will teach us of his ways, and we will walk in his paths: for out of Zion shall go forth the law, and the word of the LORD from Jerusalem."*

Not only do I think the mountains are pointing to kingdoms, but I believe the next verse in Revelation 17 gives us the key to understand this very thing. Look at the two verses together. *"9 And here is the mind which hath wisdom. The seven heads are seven mountains, on which the woman sitteth. 10 "And there are seven kings: five are fallen, and one is, and the other is not yet come; and when he cometh, he must continue a short space."(KJV)*

32

Mark(s) of the Beast

Remember at the time John was writing this it was the first century A.D. When you look at the course of human history, and the kingdoms that have brutalized God's people we see six distinct kingdoms; Egypt, Assyria, Babylon, Persia, Greece, and Rome. During John's day five were gone from the scene; Egypt, Assyria, Babylon, Persia, and Greece. However, one was still around, and that was Rome. So that explains the phrase, *"five are fallen, and one is"*. Yet, the Scriptures tells us that *"the other is not yet come, and when he cometh, he must continue a short space"*. I don't think it's a far leap to point that last one to the Anti-Christ's coming kingdom. I also don't think it is much of a stretch to realize that this last evil kingdom will have attributes of the first six, and no doubt be built upon the lessons each had learned when combating God and His people.

"Okay," you say, "If the foundation of this Anti-Christ's kingdom is built on the backs of ancient evil world kingdoms, what then can the 'ten crowns' be referring to?"

I just want to pause here to tell you that your questions just keep getting better and better. Keep up the good work!

Ten Horns and Ten Crowns

Martin W Sondermann

Crowns in Scripture usually display what you might think they do, and that is authority. I believe that in this passage this beast, whatever or whoever it is, has much authority. As for the *"ten horns"* we only have to peel away a few pages of the Bible to get that answer. In Revelation chapter 17 verse 12-13 it says; *"And the ten horns which thou sawest <u>are ten kings</u>, which have received no kingdom as yet; but receive power as kings one hour with the beast. 13 These have one mind and shall give their power and strength unto the beast."* (KJV)

So, we clearly see that those *"ten horns"* are *"ten kings."* They will receive their kingdoms in the last days and will give that <u>authority</u> over to *"the beast."* There is another passage that tells us not all of them will survive despite handing power over to the beast. In Daniel Chapter 7 verses 7 and 8 it reads; *"After this I saw in the night visions, and behold a fourth beast, dreadful and terrible, and strong exceedingly; and it had great iron teeth: it devoured and brake in pieces, and stamped the residue with the feet of it: and it was diverse from all the beasts that were before it; and <u>it had ten horns</u>. 8 I considered the horns, and, behold, there came up among them another little horn, before whom there were <u>three of the</u>*

34

first horns plucked up by the roots: and, behold, in this horn were eyes like the eyes of man, and a mouth speaking great things." (KJV)

So, we see here in Daniel chapter 7 that the Bible gives us more insight as to what is going to happen with these *"ten horns."* Daniel states that *"another little horn"* rises up among them, and *"three of the first horns"* are the *"plucked up by the roots."* Daniel describes that little horn as having *"eyes like the eyes of man, and a mouth speaking great things."* I believe this is speaking of the Anti-Christ, and I believe in some way this man of sin will be responsible for the destruction of three "kings" or world leaders. I believe that's what the term *"plucked up by the roots"* means. Think no further than your own lawn or garden. When you want to get rid of a weed once and for all you "pluck it up by the roots." That's exactly what is going to happen during the tribulation to three nations or at least those nation's leaders.

Leopards, and Bears, and Lions, oh my!

As we approach Revelation 13:2 we see another fascinating verse in our quest of 20/20 vision. *"And the beast which I saw was like unto a leopard, and his feet were as the feet of a bear, and his mouth as the mouth of a lion: and the dragon gave him his power, and his seat, and great authority." (KJV)*

Daniel chapter 7 is the cipher for this passage as well. Let's look at verses 1-7 this time. *"In the first year of Belshazzar king of Babylon Daniel had a dream and visions of his head upon his bed: then he wrote the dream and told the sum of the matters. 2 Daniel spake and said, I saw in my vision by night, and, behold, the four winds of the heaven strove upon the great sea. 3 And four great beasts came up from the sea, diverse one from another. 4 The first was like a lion and had eagle's wings: I beheld till the wings thereof were plucked, and it was lifted up from the earth, and made stand upon the feet as a man, and a man's heart was given to it. 5 And behold another beast, a second, like to a bear, and it raised up itself on one side, and it had three ribs in the mouth of it between the teeth of it: and they said thus unto it, Arise, devour much flesh. 6 After this I beheld, and lo another, like a leopard, which had upon the back of it four wings of a fowl; the beast had also four heads; and dominion was given to it. 7 After this I saw in the night visions, and behold a fourth beast, dreadful and terrible, and strong exceedingly; and it had great iron teeth: it devoured and brake in pieces, and stamped the residue with the feet of it: and it was diverse from all the beasts that were before it; and it had ten horns." (KJV)*

So, Daniel has this dream, and he sees these four beasts. Now the first three beasts he lists have a lot in common with verse 2 of Revelation 13; *"And the beast which I saw was like unto a leopard, and his feet were as the feet of a bear, and his mouth as the mouth of a lion."* If you look closely you will see that the "leopard" the "bear" and the "lion" are listed, and this correlates with Daniel chapter 7. However, something else to note is that they are in reverse order. I believe that this is critical because it tells us which side of history we are on. Let's look closer at these four beasts in Daniel 7, and try to gauge what they might be. I believe all we have to do is go back to Daniel chapter 2 for Nebuchadnezzar's dream that Daniel interprets.

Daniel's Interpretation

You might already know the story of Daniel chapter 2, but I will summarize it anyway. Daniel was serving in a pagan kingdom under a pagan king named Nebuchadnezzar. This king had a dream, but no one in his kingdom was able to tell him what the dream was, and what it meant. It says that he called on his *"magicians, astrologers, sorcerers, and the Chaldeans,"* but none could help. This made the king very angry, and he was going to have all men of counsel killed in his kingdom. This included Daniel and his friends.

However, Daniel asked the king to give him some time, and then proceeded to pray, and to have his friends pray that God would give him the dream and interpretation. God answered Daniel's prayer, and in verses 31-45 we read that this dream of Nebuchadnezzar's was about a *"great image."* It had a head of gold, breast and arms of silver, belly and thighs of brass, and legs of iron with *"his feet part of iron and part of clay."*

Daniel goes on to explain that the head of gold was Nebuchadnezzar and his Babylonian kingdom. He then states that after Babylon another inferior kingdom shall rise. Looking back through the corridor of history we know that this was speaking of the Medo-Persia kingdom. Daniel then went on to describe the third kingdom of brass, which we know was Greece. He then explains that the fourth kingdom of iron will arrive, but it will be in two sections—

or two legs. We know from history that this was the Roman Empire which was divided into two parts with one ruled by Rome, and the other ruled by Constantinople in modern day Turkey. We also must note that the feet of this image, while connected, are also a separate entity.

Daniel goes on to describe the feet and toes (10 toes) as being made from iron and clay. He states that this final kingdom will be *"partly strong, and partly broken."* This seems to be speaking of a revived Roman Empire ruled by the Anti-Christ. How do we know? Well, it is partly of iron, which described Rome, and it is attached to the description of the legs which means they are related in some way.

"Okay," you might say, "But, how do we know it's ruled by the Anti-Christ?"

Wow! Nothing gets past you does it? Great question!

How we know is because Daniel gives us the timeline. In Daniel 2 verses 43-45 it reads; *"And whereas thou sawest iron mixed with miry clay, they shall mingle themselves with the seed of men: but they shall not cleave one to another, even as iron is not mixed with clay. 44 And in the days of these kings shall the God of heaven set up a kingdom, which shall never be destroyed: and the kingdom shall not be left to other people, but it shall break in pieces and consume all these kingdoms, and it shall stand for ever. 45 Forasmuch as thou sawest that the stone was cut out of the mountain without hands, and that it brake in pieces the iron, the brass, the clay, the silver, and the gold; the great God hath made known to the king what shall come to pass hereafter: and the dream is certain, and the interpretation thereof sure.(KJV)*

Daniel states that this last kingdom will be the kingdom destroyed by Jesus at his second coming, and we know from Scripture that this lines up with the time of the Anti-Christ. I also believe the ten toes align with the ten horns in Revelation and here in Daniel. In other words, we know that **this is** the kingdom Jesus will de-feet. Get it? De-feet....

Come on, you know that was funny.

Overview

So, when you take an overview, I believe Daniel chapter 2 gives us even more insight into Daniel chapter 7. It appears to me that the four kingdoms in chapter 2 of Daniel line up with the four beasts of Daniel chapter 7. This means the final beast is the final kingdom, and when you

Mark(s) of the Beast

re-read Daniel 7 verse 7 you can see the correlation between the two with the mention of "iron" and "feet".

"After this I saw in the night visions, and behold a fourth beast, dreadful and terrible, and strong exceedingly; and it had great <u>iron</u> teeth: it devoured and brake in pieces, and stamped the residue with the <u>feet</u> of it: and it was diverse from all the beasts that were before it; and it had ten horns." (KJV)

Lost yet? I hope not. But, please be patient as we build this foundation. I believe it to be critical to understanding the power behind the coming "Marks of the Beast".

Martin W Sondermann

Chapter 3

The Making of an Evil Empire

Revelation 13:3-4

Question: What do evil empires have in common?

Answer: An evil leader.

The final world kingdom that is yet to come will indeed have at its forefront a very sinister and dark ruler. However, as Revelation 13 verse 3 indicates, it's going to appear as if that coming world leader will be cut down before he can rise to power. *3 "And I saw one of his heads as it were wounded to death; and his deadly wound was healed: and all the world wondered after the beast." (KJV)*

I believe that this verse refers to the fact that this coming world leader will experience some kind of an accident, survive some kind of attempted assassination, or suffer a great military defeat, but will rebound in a very dramatic way. Because of this fact verse 4 goes on to say, *"And they worshiped the dragon which gave power unto the beast: and they worshiped the beast, saying, Who is*

Mark(s) of the Beast

like unto the beast? who is able to make war with him?"
(KJV)

After this evil man survives this "wound", whatever it might be, the world will be in awe for some reason. This will cause "they", which refers back to *"all the world"*, to worship this man, and the god he serves, which is the dragon or Satan.

I personally think that this "wound" is a physical wound rather than something like a military defeat. The reason I say this is that there in verse 4 it says the world will say, *"who is like unto the beast? Who is able to make war with him?"* I believe that this small phrase indicates that this guy just doesn't seem like he can lose a war or a battle, at least until the final battle. I am not dogmatic about it, but it's where my opinion is as I write this book. I think maybe he survives an assassination attempts or something like it, and because it's so dramatic it captivates the world.

Revelation 13:5-6

Nevertheless, after this *"wound was healed"*, and the world begins to worship this beast verses 5-6 tells us what he does next. *"And there was given unto him a mouth speaking great things and blasphemies; and power was*
Martin W Sondermann

given unto him to continue forty and two months. 6 And he opened his mouth in blasphemy against God, to blaspheme his name, and his tabernacle, and them that dwell in heaven. (KJV)

A Big Mouth

This evil dictator has a big mouth, and he uses it to brag and speak blasphemies. Notice first that he blasphemes God, His tabernacle, and *"them that dwell in heaven."* I personally believe that the blasphemy directed toward those in Heaven is a reference to those who have departed in the Rapture.

The Rapture

A side note about the Rapture. I personally don't believe Christians will physically disappear. It is my opinion, and I am not dogmatic about this, but it is my opinion that we leave our physical bodies behind. I think there is no reason to take our corrupted flesh into the Kingdom of God, and I believe we will receive a perfect eternal body at the moment of the Rapture and leave our old sinful carcass lying on the ground. But, again, that's another study for another day.

Mark(s) of the Beast

Getting back to the Anti-Christ blaming those departed, I think this verse in Revelation 13 tells us that during the tribulation the Anti-Christ will mock and blaspheme those taken up. I think he will make up some story as to what happened all over the globe, and he may even somehow blame those taken for all the world's current problems. Understand that word for blasphemies is "blasphemia" in the Greek. It simply means to vilify or speak evil of. So, apparently this evil ruler will use the same thing Hitler and other evil leaders have used, and that is to vilify a segment of society as to unify others against them. But, as we keep reading, we see that he's not only going to vilify those departed, he is also going to focus his evil gaze on some left behind.

God's People: Revelation 13:7

Revelation 13 verse 7 tells us who the Anti-Christ will attack; *"And it was given unto him to make war with the saints, and to overcome them: and power was given him over all kindreds, and tongues, and nations." (KJV)*

Notice that this evil leader goes after "the saints". These are the tribulation saints, probably mostly Jewish, but a fair number of gentiles will no doubt be part of this group as

Martin W Sondermann

well. As mentioned, a few times previously, I believe the Church will already be taken out via the Rapture. According to the Scriptures believers during the tribulation are a separate work of God than His Church that was taken in the Rapture. This is why the Anti-Christ can defeat tribulation saints even though Scripture gives the Church the promise that Satan will never prevail against it. To give some context look at Matthew chapter 16 when Jesus states that He will establish His Church, and *"the gates of Hell will not prevail against it"*. In contrast to this we see that the Anti-Christ will indeed have power given to him by God to overcome the *"saints"*. Another passage to note is 1 Thessalonians chapter 5 verse 9 when it tells us that God didn't appoint the Church unto wrath, and yet we know from the first set of plagues in Revelation chapter 6 God's wrath is exactly what is being poured out on the entire world. This would include the tribulation saints, who, once again, I believe are different than the Church. Revelation 6:17, *"For the great day of his wrath is come; and who shall be able to stand?" (KJV)*

Mark(s) of the Beast

God is allowing this arrogant, blasphemous, evil dictator to overcome the saints, but make no mistake; everything will still be under God's control, even if it doesn't appear so at the time.

The False Prophet: Revelation 13:8-14

During the last 42 months of the Anti-Christ reign the world will line up to worship this man. *8 "And all that dwell upon the earth <u>shall worship him</u>, whose names are not written in the book of life of the Lamb slain from the foundation of the world.9 If any man have an ear, let him hear.10 He that leadeth into captivity shall go into captivity: he that killeth with the sword must be killed with the sword. Here is the patience and the faith of the saints." (KJV)*

Unholy Trinity

But just so you know, this coming world leader will not do it all on his own. In a mirrored counterfeit in opposition to the Holy Trinity, this brutal butcher will have the help of the false god Satan, and of the false spiritual leader known to many in Christian circles as the "false prophet". Starting at verse 11, *"And I beheld another beast coming up out of the earth; and he had two horns like a lamb, and he spake as a dragon." (KJV)*

Another beast is going to rise up out of the earth. Some scholars suggest that the word "earth" is a reference to the Jewish nation. In the same way "the sea" relates to gentile nations. However, I have yet to find a real connection to that theory personally. But we do know that this second beast does have horns like a lamb, which could be an indication that there may be a religious connection to "Christianity" because of the lamb imagery. A good lesson for all of us to remember is that no matter how much a person looks like a lamb their heart is always revealed through the words they speak, and through their actions. This man here verse 11 speaks as a dragon, and we know his actions will be evil. In my opinion this points to a religious leader that claims Christianity, but the things he will say are going to be contrary to the Scriptures. This fake believer will rise up to help the Anti-Christ gain a foothold in the world. I believe this liar could also assure the world that what has occurred previously on the planet is not the event known as "the Rapture." I believe he will help to explain it away. He will most likely inject into the dialogue plausible explanations such as aliens were involved, or perhaps some new kind of disease, or maybe he will insist that the planet or environment, or better yet, "Mother Nature" defended herself. After all, it couldn't have been the Rapture because there will be many "so-called" Christians still around including this one who has the horns of a lamb but speaks like a dragon.

This fake lamb will be more like a ravenous wolf helping to devour those who oppose the Anti-Christ's kingdom. This would include the destruction of tribulation saints. So, if this evil False-Prophet is a fake Christian, he will no doubt find a reason to claim the tribulation saints are actually the enemies of "god" or at least "his god." *Verse 12 "And he exerciseth all the power of the first beast before him, and causeth the earth and them which dwell therein to worship the first beast, whose deadly wound was healed." (KJV)*

But, why will so many listen to this liar? The Bible tells us here in the next two verses, *13 "And he doeth great wonders, so that he maketh fire come down from heaven on the earth in the sight of men, 14 And deceiveth them that dwell on the earth by the means of those miracles which he had power to do in the sight of the beast; saying to them that dwell on the earth, that they should make an image to the beast, which had the wound by a sword, and did live. (KJV)*

Miracles Don't Mean Godly

This False-Prophet is going to fool so many by the actual miracles he is able to perform. Here is another huge warning for all believers, even in this current age. Just because someone displays signs and wonders or miracles, it doesn't mean they are "of God". In fact, a good rule of thumb I heard a Pastor once say is that believers should never follow after signs and wonders. Instead, signs and wonders should follow believers as they minister and preach the Gospel. Just look at how powerful signs and wonders can be. They can be a very powerful force, and as we see here in verses 13 and 14, they can indeed be duplicated by the enemy. I wonder how many so called "TV preachers" have been gifted by a different god? I wonder how many self-proclaimed miracle workers obtain their power from a false god? We as Christians should be wise as serpents and gentle as doves. We should indeed test all things.

Chapter 4

The Image

Works of Their Hands

Isn't it amazing how nearly every form of false worship leads to the creation of some sort of image to go along with it? If you read historical accounts from around the world there seems to be a common connection between false teaching, false worship, and the creation of false gods in the form of vain images. Even within the pages of the Bible we see this play out. In Exodus 32 we read about the Children of Israel while trying to make their way to the Promised Land became impatient waiting for their leader Moses to return from the mountain top. As a result of their impatience they demanded that Aaron create for them an image to worship. In reading this account I find it very interesting the way they ask him to do this evil thing. I think it gives us real insight into their character. The first part of verse 1 in Exodus 32 says, *"And when the people saw that Moses delayed to come down out of the mount, the people gathered themselves together unto Aaron, and said unto him, Up, make us gods, which shall go before us; (KJV)*

In this verse the people *"gathered themselves together".* Notice, they didn't go to Aaron individually. They didn't pull him aside and say, "hey Aaron, you know what we really need is a golden god to worship." No, instead they gathered together, and with strength in numbers began to demand something to worship. Also notice that it seems as if some form of fear is involved, *"make us gods, which shall go before us."* If you read back in Exodus 14 when the Israelites were about to cross the Red Sea, we find out that the Angel of the LORD went before them. However, now, since they weren't seeing the progress, they desired they wanted something, anything to lead them, to go before them.

Still Preaching

This is why we as Christians need to be very careful about not allowing something to be accepted just because a large number, even a majority of people, think it's okay. As believers we must test everything with the Scripture and the Holy Spirit. How many crazy doctrines have slithered their way into the Church just because one group decided it was true and right? It is an area that all of us need to be careful of. Again, test all things, hold fast to that which is good.

Not only that, but we also need to be absolutely cautious in the area of "getting something done for God." How many ministries are started because someone thinks it's a "good idea" without stopping and praying to find out if it's a "God idea?" How much "false fire" is generated inside the church in the name of progress motivated by the fear of "not doing something?" I've seen it so much in Christian ministry. People make up ideas just to fill the time, or just because they think they "need to do something." I suggest the "thing" we all need to do is pray, study, and wait for the Lord to lead. Do not become impatient just because the Lord isn't coming down off the mountain fast enough for you. But, it is equally important not to delay once the Lord makes something clear. Imagine if this group in Exodus would have just waited a bit longer for Moses. They would have been blessed, and the commandments given would have sparked something beautiful. Instead death entered their camp.

Martin W Sondermann

Idol Worship Always Brings Death

The rest of the story doesn't end well for many of the individuals written about in Exodus chapter 32. The Scripture explains to us that about 3,000 of those of who begged for their golden god, and were happily dancing naked around it, were slain for their actions. This reminds us that ALL false worship leads to some kind of death. It can be the death of relationships. It can be the death of truth. It can be the death of humility. It can be the death of innocence. However, ultimately anyone who puts their faith and trust in a false god, and worships a false god, will find their physical death will also lead to their spiritual death. There is no way around it, and there is no way to come back from that. Exodus 32, Verses 27 and 28 read; *"And he said unto them, Thus saith the LORD God of Israel, Put every man his sword by his side, and go in and out from gate to gate throughout the camp, and slay every man his brother, and every man his companion, and every man his neighbour. 28 And the children of Levi did according to the word of Moses: and there fell of the people that day about three thousand men." (KJV)*

Idol Worship Always Brings Perversion

Something else to note about this story is that Idol worship usually leads to some kind of perversion. These Israelites demanded a golden god, and then began to dance naked around it. This is not normal behavior. You see, that's what happens to any of us if we get off track. If we begin to worship false gods we will become perverted in some way. That perversion is not always sexual, but often times it is. The reason is because we will do anything we can to fill the void that false worship creates. We crave satisfaction in the flesh because we are unable to be content in the spiritual. It is the battle we all face and remember not all false gods are golden. I am sure all of us, if we are honest, can find areas in our lives that have been given some form of false worship. If we are honest, we all have things that need to be cut out of our lives. It is something every non-Christian and Christian struggles with. It is also an area that invites demonic oppression and harassment. You give the enemy a foothold in your life, and he is happy to run with it.

This human condition that causes most people to chase after things to worship is going to be exploited heavily by the False-Prophet and the Anti-Christ system. During the tribulation an idol is going to be commissioned like no other idol that has ever existed. It too will lead to the perversion of the people, and ultimately death for many. However, it will be much more than just 3,000 souls. It will be a great portion of the world's population in those days, and eventually all that worship it will find their place in Hell forever.

Back on Track: Revelation 13:14-15

In the previous chapter of this book we looked at one part of Revelation 13 verse 14, but now we are going to focus on the last part of that verse, and the verse to follow because both have a key to this coming deception. *"And deceiveth them that dwell on the earth by the means of those miracles which he had power to do in the sight of the beast; saying to them that dwell on the earth, that they should make an image to the beast, which had the wound by a sword, and did live.15 And he had power to give life unto the image of the beast, that the image of the beast should both speak, and cause that as many as would not worship the image of the beast should be killed." (KJV)*

These miracles that the False-Prophet is able to perform lead to action. It is going to cause people from all over the

56

earth to worship an image. Not only that, but anyone who refuses to do so is going to be hunted down and killed.

It Lives!

Notice an astonishing thing about this evil created image. The False-Prophet is given power to "give life" to this image. Let that sink in. This image, whatever it is, becomes alive. Not fake life, not imagined life, but real, honest to goodness breathe of life type of living. These are very specific words used here by the Holy Spirit writing this book through the Apostle John.

An image, which is defined by the Merriam-Webster Dictionary[iv]as; *"a reproduction or imitation of the form of a person or thing; especially : an imitation in solid form (statue)"*. It also says; *"a visual representation of something."*

According to Strong's Concordance[v] the Greek word used for the word "image" used in verse 15 is "eikon". It is pronounced i-kone', and it means *"a likeness, that is, literally statue, profile, or figuratively representation, resemblance, image"*.

Make no mistake this is something that is created by the hands of man, and yet it becomes alive!

In Psalm 115 the Bible speaks about the types of idols men make in place of God. In Verses 2 through 8 it reads; *"Wherefore should the heathen say, Where is now their God? 3 But our God is in the heavens: he hath done whatsoever he hath pleased. 4 Their idols are silver and gold, the work of men's hands. 5 They have mouths, but they speak not: eyes have they, but they see not: 6 They have ears, but they hear not: noses have they, but they smell not: 7 They have hands, but they handle not: feet have they, but they walk not: neither speak they through their throat. 8 They that make them are like unto them; so is every one that trusteth in them."* (KJV)

Here it tells us that all the idols of gold and silver that men create with their own hands, they can't speak, they can't see, they can't hear, they can't handle, and they can't walk. However, this image that the False-Prophet will raise up is different than any other idol that came before it. It has life—literal life. The Greek word used there to describe life is "pneuma". It is pronounced new-ma, and according to Strong's Concordance it is defined as, *"a current of air, that*

58

is, breath, or a breeze, by analogy or figuratively a spirit". It goes on to further describe it as; *"human the rational soul, by implication vital principle, mental disposition, etc., or superhuman an angel, demon, or divine God, Christ's spirit, the Holy Spirit, ghost, life, spiritual, spiritually, mind".* No pun intended, but this definition should blow your mind. Not only that, but it should also remind you of another verse in the Bible all the way back in Genesis.

Since we know that the Anti-Christ, and False-Prophet prophet are going to be fueled by the king of all liars and deceivers it should be no huge surprise that Satan would try to counterfeit everything God does. When we look back at Genesis chapter 2 verse 7 during the time of creation, we see that God the Father gave life to Adam with breath. That verse reads; **"And the LORD God formed man of the dust of the ground, and breathed into his nostrils the <u>breath of life</u>; and man became a <u>living soul</u>" (KJV)**

Remember also that man is created "in the image of God." Jump to the other end of the Bible in the book of Revelation chapter 13, and we see Satan somehow giving the ability to this False-Prophet to give life, "pneuma", breath, perhaps even a soul to this "image of the beast". Maybe it's a resurrected soul from Hell? Nimrod? Hitler?

Martin W Sondermann

Judas? Nero? A fallen angel? Or, maybe it's the soul of the Anti-Christ that is transferred somehow? Or, it could be someone or something completely different. Regardless of this we know that the image will have life. It will have the breath of life derived somehow from an evil source and looking at the definition of pneuma the phrase "superhuman an angel, demon", seems to jump off the page considering what this "thing" will be able to do.

Chapter 5

Constructing a god

The Future is Now

The days we find ourselves living in are truly amazing. The advancements in science, technology, and information are absolutely staggering. It's also absolutely terrifying.

Before diving into this section, it must be noted that I am not claiming that any of the technologies or companies in this chapter will be actively involved in assisting the Anti-Christ or the False-Prophet. All I am trying to do set the table for the reasonable mind to understand the days in which we live.

For instance, did you know that scientists have been working on, and have actually created, a partially synthetic life-form? It was announced in 2017 that scientists had made this major breakthrough. These scientists created a bacterium that uses four natural base pairs and one pair of synthetic DNA. These researchers believe they have been able to pave the way for creating 100% synthetic biology.

Another amazing breakthrough in this area was reported in 2019 that scientists have actually done

Martin W Sondermann

something absolutely mind boggling. It seems they have created machines that act as close to lifelike as you can get. From my understanding they have been working in the area of robotics, and have created a DNA partnership with technology. They have engineered what is essentially an organic bridge with robotics that will not only act as if it is alive, but it will also expire, or basically die.

Now, I am not a scientist, and I don't even play one on TV. But I am a Christian, and I find all of this a bit overwhelming. It reminds me of a joke I once heard about a group of scientists that came to God one day and said, "We have advanced so much in the area of science and technology that we can do anything you can do God. In fact, we are so confident in our abilities that after reading your account in Genesis we believe we can build a better human than you can."

Without skipping a beat God said, "Okay, you go first."

The lead scientist grinned, and then bent over to gather soil to start his process. However, before he was able to really get started God stopped him and simply said, "Hey, get your own dirt."

The story is funny, but very profound. Some in the scientific community are attempting to play God, but may not realize, or are just not interested in, their finite capacity. Of course, that is painting with a broad brush, and I am sure that not all are willing to jump so quickly into areas that we ought not jump. Still, there do seem to be a large number of researchers who have no issue with tinkering with creation.

CRISPR

Another example of incredible advancements can be found in something called CRISPR. It is pronounced "crisper" and stands for "Clustered Regularly Interspaced Short Palindromic Repeats." Say that five times fast.

This technology is remarkable, and no doubt can help a lot of people. What it can do, is go in and alter the DNA of a person to clean up bad DNA and replace it with good. Or, at least that's my limited understanding. Again, on the surface level this technology sounds promising, and it must be noted that I am not a Luddite. I am not opposed to advancements in technology or science. In fact, I find all of it fascinating, and I would whole-heartily embrace almost any ethical medical advancement that helps save lives and improve the quality of living. But these advancements should come only within certain boundaries, and I know that most companies utilizing this kind of technology would agree.

Now, I have my own list of guidelines I think should be followed in these areas. I don't put them on others, but I think it's a good list. First, any technology must not harm some to save others. Second, it must not be experimented on those who do not know, have not volunteered, or been willingly compensated for testing. Lastly, it should not put human beings in jeopardy from being wiped off the face of the planet because someone forgot to carry a one, flipped the wrong switch, or decided that they needed prime real estate being occupied by those deemed undesirable. And, as much as that all sounds like hyperbole, the fact remains that advanced technology in the wrong hands can be devastatingly dangerous.

I am sure the motivation of those who have created the CRISPR technology and other similar breakthroughs are noble. However, what happens when that same technology falls into the hands of those who don't care about ethics, the greater good, or what might happen to the masses if used incorrectly? But this may be an even bigger question when it comes to the topic of artificial intelligence.

The Robots Might Take Over

Mark(s) of the Beast

Artificial Intelligence or "AI" is something that is going to be discussed much more in the near future. The advancements in this area are fascinating. If you read the news on this topic you will find that nearly every company in the field of technology and computers is currently experimenting and attempting to improve some form of AI. The country of China is really pushing this trend, and probably are becoming the world's leader.

Google is planning a huge project based on making AI more user-friendly and useful for the average person. Facebook has jumped into this field as well, and they have a project called "FAIR", and it stands for "Facebook Artificial Intelligence Researchers". Other companies heavily invested in AI technologies are the usual, Apple, Microsoft, and IBM. One of the biggest names that you may not have heard of is a company called DeepMind. They were acquired by Google in 2014, but still hold on to their own identity. They are based in London, and they believe that A.I. may be able to one day solve the world's most complex problems. And, while this might sound like a bold idea, just think of how incredible it would be. I mean, imagine a computer that can solve the most difficult problems in the world, things like hunger, war, famine,

Martin W Sondermann

pollution, it would be amazing. Wouldn't it be? Wouldn't that just be incredible? Who could have ever predicted such a thing?

Let's just hope this technology they have created has a built in auto-destruct button. Let's also hope that if this AI gets out of control it isn't so smart that it can turn its own auto-destruct button off—against the wishes of its creator. I think we've all seen the movies. It doesn't end well.

If you are concerned about AI like I am, just know that we aren't alone. One of the most well-known scientists in the world, the late Professor Stephen Hawking, shared his concerns about this emerging technology. He was quoted by the BBC[vi] in saying, *"the development of full artificial intelligence could spell the end of the human race."*

Oh, is that all?

Hawking's words are not the majority opinion on this, but he is certainly not the only prominent figure concerned with this technology. Tesla CEO Elon Musk has also made his reservations of AI well known. However, the solution he offers might be just as frightening. He was quoted as saying[vii], *"Over time I think we will probably see a closer merger of biological intelligence and digital intelligence."* He told this to a group at the World Government Summit in

Mark(s) of the Beast

Dubai. Musk went on to explain that humans must merge with machines so that we do not become irrelevant in an age of Artificial Intelligence. He went on to note the dangerous situation humans will find themselves in if AI is *"smarter than the smartest human on earth."* According to Elon if humans don't upgrade, they may find themselves obsolete. The answer for him is trans-humanism technologies which provide all of us the means to keep up with the exponential growth.

Trans-humanism: It's Not What You Think

Trans-humanism, if you don't know, is an area of science and technology that is working hard to combine human beings with hardware upgrades. It is related to AI but focuses more on upgrading you and I. Things like mind uploads and using cybernetics to develop technologies that create artificial body parts, and upgrades. How about installing nanobots in your blood supply to fix things? Or, what about injecting them into your body to perform surgery? What about connecting your newly upgraded mind to a collective web that unites all of us with thought and purpose? Far-fetched? Perhaps, but Revelation 13 seems to indicate the image created by the False-Prophet will be connected to those who worship it in some way. Perhaps it

Martin W Sondermann

will merely be the Internet, or a new form of internet powered by super computers. Who really knows?

Quantum Computing

Speaking of super computers, I wonder if you have ever heard of D-Wave? D-Wave is an amazing company that has pioneered the area of quantum computing. In trying to explain what quantum computers are, D-Wave Co-Founder Geordie Rose in a video posted on YouTube[viii] told the group he was speaking to that these computers are doing something "completely different." He goes on to explain that these computers have, "access to new resources," and then he actually calls these new resources "parallel universes", and that's not a typo. NASA is using these computers, and so is Google. In fact, these two have united to create a quantum computing AI laboratory using D-Wave technology. Rose goes on to describe the performance of these computers and starts by explaining the pulse they emit is "eerily like a heartbeat." He then actually stated that standing next to one of these D-Wave computers, feels like standing next to "the altar to an alien god."

Chip off the New Block

What powers this computer? It is a small chip about the size of a thumbnail that allows something to happen that isn't easily described with our current English vocabulary. He describes a concept in quantum mechanics that says a thing can exist in "two states at the same time." He then explains to the crowd the power behind it all is something called a "qubit" or a "quantum bit."

He continues his description of a qubit claiming it is, "like a bit or a transistor in a conventional computer." But there seems to be one big difference. He then explains that conventional computers have "two distinct physical states which we call 0 and 1." In other words, in a regular computer something is either 0 or 1, it's either on or off. It's not both at the same time.

Rose then blows the minds of those listening when he explains a quantum computer using this qubit technology has the unique ability to, "be in this strange situation where these two parallel universes have a nexus, a point in space where they overlap." He goes on to explain one of D-Wave's goals with this computer. "The way I think about it is that the shadows of these parallel worlds overlap with ours, and if we're smart enough we can dive into them and grab their resources and pull them back into ours to make an effect in our world." And, if you think he's exaggerating or being dramatic he quickly explains that he is not, in fact he states, "I am using language that a normal theoretical physicist probably wouldn't use, but this is, what I'm telling you, is absolutely correct and in line with the way that these things actually work." He goes on to give a timeline of their progress explaining that the doubling of this technology has happened, "once a year for the past nine years."

Again, I am not a physicist, and we have already established that I am not a scientist. But, from my understanding this computer somehow creates nexus that allows two things to be in the same space at the same time. It is not a conventional binary based computer. It's not a 0 or a 1; it's a 0 and a 1 at the same time. It's on and it's off all at once. It's a particle and a wave simultaneously. From more study of this computer I have also learned that it doesn't necessarily work in linear time like other standard computers. In other words, a standard PC thinks linearly. It may be able to compute thousands of choices one-after-another in a matter of seconds, but it still had to process those computations in order, in linear time. However, this quantum computer isn't necessarily hindered by that kind of processing. It can somehow process multiple solutions at the same time. It's on, it's off, it's on, it's a 1, it's a 0, it's a 1 all at the same time, and it can think of multiple solutions simultaneously. Again, not an expert, this is just my understanding from my reading and listening to these explanations, but it almost does sounds like some kind of alien god.

A New Kind of Web

Of course, a super computer that can have the ability to be almost all knowing, and control so much, would be limited by not being able to be all places at one time. But what if that computer was tied into a super web that was connected to every camera and microphone with an IP address? This would include every smartphone, the latest televisions, microwaves, ovens, refrigerators, washing machines, automobiles, and the list goes on-and-on. What if it had access to all banking, every sale, and every single electronic transaction? What if it also had a way to peer down from space at any moment, and at any location on the planet? Sound crazy? It really isn't considering the days in which we now live. In fact, did you know there is a joint project between SpaceX and a company called OneWeb that is currently producing a new form of satellite internet? They have already begun to produce thousands of small satellites in the state of Florida that will be launched into low-earth orbit in the coming years. From what I understand, the group is planning to launch some of these satellites initially, and have full coverage of the planet within the next five years or so. This will be the backbone for a brand-new kind of internet provider. This will not be limited by cables, digging trenches, etc. It will give the web global coverage anywhere the sky can be seen. Imagine the possibilities. In February of 2019 OneWeb had its first successful launch with more in the works.

5G You and Me

So, now that 5G Technology is upon us I guess we should ask, what is it? If you don't know about it, or haven't heard about it, then you're really not any less informed about it than most people who have. 5G Technology is set to revolutionize the way we communicate. If you thought your phone and internet were impressive now. Just wait and see what 5G brings. The possibilities are mind boggling. 5G promises to be over 40 times faster than the current 4G system, and it will open up more usages such as augmented reality, artificial intelligence, virtual reality, gaming, etc.

Collision Course

Another technological advancement in the world that should be mentioned is the Large Hadron Collider (LHC) located beneath the France and Switzerland border near Geneva, Switzerland. The LHC is operated by CERN, which is the European Organization for Nuclear Research. The LHC is the world's biggest particle accelerator, and the project consists of a 27-kilometer ring lined with magnets and technologies that help to accelerate particles and experiment with the collision of those particles together. What makes this particularly interesting for our subject matter is that some of the experiments they are doing at CERN with the LHC are focused on finding and accessing other dimensions, and even perhaps creating small versions of black holes.

Things Are Lining Up

So why would any of this be related to Anti-Christ technology or the Image of the Beast created by the False-Prophet? Well, it's not. Because that kingdom is still yet to come. However, some kind of technology will have to be utilized in the future, and all the talk of parallel universes, black holes, world-wide internet coverage from the sky, super powered life-like computers, artificial intelligence and everything else to go along with it, sure tells me we are living in interesting times. The same "times" that the Bible predicted just before the return of Christ.

Martin W Sondermann

The Bible Tells Me So

From a Biblical perspective we know that Satan and the fallen angels dwell primarily in another dimension. They do seem to be inter-dimensional in that they can interact in the spiritual realm with humans on a regular basis.

There also seems to be a limitation to that interaction. Demons do not seem to be able to readily move into the physical realm without a host. But, this changes during the tribulation.

We know that during the tribulation period the Anti-Christ and False-Prophet will have supernatural powers and be aided by demonic forces. We also know a very unique "living" image is going to be created. So, what if these "champions" of Satan were able to utilize some kind of technology to readily communicate with malevolent spiritual powers?

What if they are able to gain power and strength like never seen before through the union of demonic and physical armies? What if they were able to summon things that can only be imagined in horror stories and science fiction? What if they are able to create a living image that is connected to all things electronic, and it gives it unmatched

Mark(s) of the Beast

power and force? I tell you one thing, I don't want to be
here to find out.

Martin W Sondermann

Chapter 6

The Number of Man

The infamous number 6-6-6 is a number that has been feared, researched, mocked, and speculated over for about nineteen-hundred years. It has been the source of many movies, books, documentaries, studies, myths, jokes, and some really bad tattoos. It is a number that many know about and yet a number that seems to have only grown in mystery over the centuries. In the last verse of Revelation 13 we read, *"Here is wisdom. Let him that hath understanding count the number of the beast: for it is the number of a man; and his number is <u>Six hundred threescore and six</u>." (KJV)*

From the way I see it there are three major points in this verse that must be addressed. First, what does it mean when it says, *"let him that hath understanding count the number of the beast"*? Second, what does it mean when it says, *"For it is the number of a man"*? Lastly, what does the number *"Six hundred threescore and six"*, or 6-6-6 mean?

Mark(s) of the Beast

Why is it Man's Number?

Let's look by trying to understand the last two questions first. Many Biblical scholars have pointed out that the number 6 by itself is recognized as the number of man. Not the number of a man mind you, but simply the number of mankind. The reason behind that is threefold. First, man was created on the 6th day of creation. Also, man was told that he would work 6 days, and then rest on the 7th. Lastly, and probably most important is that 6 is one number short of 7, and while that doesn't take a rocket scientist to figure out, that small difference is huge in the Kingdom of God.

You see the number 7 is referred to by many of those same scholars as God's number, or God's perfect number. After all, God rested on the 7th day of creation. Each week has 7 days. There are 7 continents, and 7 oceans. Not only that, but if you look at the book of Revelation you see that there are the 7 Churches, 7 Letters, 7 golden lamp-stands, 7 angels 7 spirits of God, 7 seals, 7 trumpets, 7 vials or bowls, and 7 stars. This doesn't even begin to account for how many times the number 7 is mentioned throughout the entire Bible over 450 other times.

The False Trinity

Martin W Sondermann

This one number difference is a big deal when you consider that during the tribulation period Satan will create his own counterfeit trinity. When we think of the perfect Holy Trinity, we know that it consists of the Father, Son, and Holy Spirit. During the last 7 years of history prior to Jesus setting up His Kingdom here on earth we know that there will be a false trinity on the scene. This evil trio will consist of the Dragon, who is Satan, and he will be in the role of the false father. You might even consider him the Anti-Father. We also know that the Beast, or Anti-Christ, is exactly that. He will be the false Christ, or literally "against or instead of Christ". Lastly, we know that the False-Prophet will be on the scene spreading his spiritual message of a one-world religion, and you can think of him as the Anti-Spirit. These three will be nothing like the real thing, and when you consider that 7 is God's perfect number, and that 6 is the number of man, it isn't much of a stretch to see how 6-6-6 would line up with a false trinity.

Another interesting fact about the number 6-6-6 being the number of a man, and 6 being the number of man or (mankind) is found in the periodic table. Mankind is a carbon-based life form. Biblical scholars would contend that mankind is actually <u>the ultimate carbon-based life form</u>

that God Almighty has created. When you look at the periodic table, we find a very curious thing about carbon. Not only is Carbon's atomic number 6, but within each carbon atom are 6 protons, 6 neutrons, and 6 electrons. No, we are all not the "Beast". But you have to admit this is quite interesting.

Searching the Scriptures for 6-6-6

When searching out the understanding of anything within the pages of the Bible the best place to look for answers is the Bible itself. I addressed this already, but it bears repeating. In looking at other passages in the Bible as a way to better understand what 6-6-6 is, and how it could relate to a "man" we do find that this number has been used before. In 1 Kings Chapter 10 the Bible gives us an overview of the splendor of King Solomon, and as part of that description it tells us how much money Solomon was paid yearly. Verse 14 reads, ***"The weight of the gold that Solomon received yearly was 666 talents."(KJV)***

I think there are two things to point out about this verse. First, I find it very interesting that God chose to mention this specific number in the Bible, and that it definitely points to a system of commerce. The curious thing about the amount though is that this wasn't all the money that

Solomon received during a year. The very next verse says, *15 "Not including the revenues from merchants and traders and from all the Arabian kings and the governors of the territories.(KJV)* So God, in His infinite wisdom chose to tell us that Solomon received 666 talents of gold per year, but that didn't include a lot of other gold he received. Whenever I see things like this in the Bible, I pay attention. It seems to me that God went out of his way to relate this number to a king with supernatural wisdom, and a specific amount of gold which points to a monetary or economic system.

Remember Solomon was the son of King David, and when God asked him what he desired Solomon answered wisely, no pun intended. Okay, pun intended. In any case, Solomon asked God for wisdom and knowledge, and God granted him with it above any other man. Of course, I am oversimplifying the story, but in a nut shell that's what happened.

Anyone who has studied the Bible or heard of Solomon knows that he was known around the world for his wisdom and knowledge. His kingdom was without equal. He was wealthy beyond imagination. He was able to construct great things and lead vast numbers of people. He was known for his wise solutions to problems, inventions, and decisions. The whole world marveled at Solomon, and so will they marvel at the Anti-Christ.

I believe the Beast will in many ways be like Solomon. He will be a king that people revere. He will solve many of the world's problems and issues. I also believe he will find a solution to control all commerce and feed the world's population with the system he will create. He will also oversee the building of the Jewish Temple—just like Solomon. The Anti-Christ will be like Solomon in so many ways, but once again, he will only be a counterfeit at best. However, his wisdom and knowledge will not come from God, but instead will be derived from Satan himself.

I find it equally intriguing that the last verse in Revelation 13 starts with, *"Here is wisdom. Let him that hath understanding count the number of the beast."* Solomon was known for wisdom, and I wonder if this was a hint at the number that followed?

Math Class

So, what does it mean to say, *"Let him that hath understanding count the number of the beast"?* Some scholars claim that this is telling us that somehow the number of the beast will calculate out the letters of a specific man's name. This can be done through the practice of "gematria".

"Gema what?" You might ask.

Gematria, pronounced (ga-may-tree-uh), is an ancient method of calculation utilizing the letters in the Hebrew alphabet each having a set numeric value. It is a very old method that some suggest came out of the Kabbalistic tradition. If you don't know what that is it's really okay. The Kabbalistic tradition is derived from the practice known as Kabbalah which is derived from Jewish mysticism. The word itself means "to receive" or "receive tradition". Kabbalah has many different traditions and thoughts, but its foundation is the mystical interpretation of spiritual things. For the record I do not recommend that Christians study or have anything to do with Kabbalah. There are so many different schools of thought within this tradition, and much of what is taught is contrary to the Holy Bible. I must also mention that there are those that suggest the practice of assigning numbers to Hebrew letters came along even

Mark(s) of the Beast

before Kabbalah. I personally don't know for sure, so I am careful with my limited understanding.

There is another interesting note on gematria as it pertains to the value of each of the Hebrew letters. Or, at least I find it interesting. In gematria each letter has a numerical value, as mentioned, and the sixth letter in ancient Hebrew is the "Waw". A quick note about this; I am only speaking of ancient Hebrew for this example. The ancient Hebrew is the language the Old Testament was written in, and just so we are clear, I am not talking about modern Hebrew. In any case, in ancient Hebrew the letter "Waw" or "Vav", was and is the 6th letter, and it has a value of 6. When you look at the ancient Hebrew letter Waw, it can be utilized as the "W" sound. Therefore, it creates a strange relationship with the term used to connect every modern website, in other words "WWW." Again, not going to write about a book about this connection, not even going to spend a lot of time on it, but it is very interesting to me that a "World Wide Web" would be connected with the Hebrew value of 6-6-6 or W-W-W. Just something interesting to chew on.

Now, one of the biggest problem with trying to use gematria in trying to figure out who the Anti-Christ is, is

Martin W Sondermann

that it is based on the Hebrew alphabet, and not the Greek alphabet, which is what the New Testament was mostly written in. But there is a very similar Greek language practice called "Isopephy". Over the centuries scholars and religious zealots have used both gematria and isopephy to attempt to figure out which historical figure might be the Anti-Christ. In fact, some scholars who believe nearly everything in the Book of Revelation has already come to pass, point to the work done to calculate Caesar Nero's name with the number 6-6-6. It must be noted that Nero's name doesn't calculate 6-6-6 in the Greek method. It first has to be translated into Hebrew, and then calculated using the Hebrew method of gematria. Doing this "Nero Caesar" calculates 6-6-6. But one other thing that must be recognized is that this number is the "number of a man", and nowhere does it say it will be his name and the title of his office. "Caesar" is Nero's title, and his full name is actually Nero Claudius Caesar Augustus Germanicus. You are more than welcome to go do that calculation on your own. I will just wait over here.

My personal opinion, and that's all it is, is that like many Biblical prophecies the truth will not be completely understood until the event happens. I do believe that

84

followers of Jesus who become believers during the tribulation might just be able to "calculate" this number out in some way. I am not sure how, and I don't want to be here to find out.

I also don't believe all of Revelation has already happened as some suggest. If for no other reason that Jesus spoke of that time of tribulation in Matthew 24 verse 21 as being the worst the world will ever know, *"For then shall be great tribulation, such as was not since the beginning of the world to this time, no, nor ever shall be." (KJV)* If you do a complete study of Revelation you will see that the dramatic devastating events described have in no way come to pass. The horrible plagues and events coming upon the earth in that time-period are beyond anything that has ever occurred on this planet short of the great flood. For anyone to say that this happened in the first century I just can't agree with them in any way. I think World War I and II alone, which took place in the twentieth century, were far worse than what occurred in the first century. I also think a myriad of wars, murderous dictators, famines, and natural disasters over the last nineteen hundred years probably pale what happened during that early time period following the time of Christ.

Martin W Sondermann

Chapter 7

Multiple Marks?

Review

Here is what we know so far; there will be a one-world government that will be formed. It will start with 10 nations, but 3 of those nations will be subdued, or "plucked up by the roots". This kingdom will be like the previous 6 kingdoms that ruled over the earth and persecuted God's people. We also know this evil kingdom will be of the six, but it will be the seventh.

The Anti-Christ will rise up to rule over this powerful kingdom, and he will be aided by the False-Prophet and Satan himself. They will form a false trinity and bring the world to submission. The False-Prophet will be able to perform miracles that cause people to worship the Anti-Christ, and not only that, he will create a "living" image that the world will be in awe of. This image will somehow be given life, and it will attempt to kill anyone that doesn't worship it. We also know that this evil trio will be given power to kill millions, which includes new believers in Jesus Christ. This Anti-Christ figure will be revered, and

Mark(s) of the Beast

much like Solomon he will seem to have answers to many of the world's most difficult issues, including the Jerusalem issue and the Jewish Temple. People will marvel at his kingdom, and even ask *"Who is like unto the beast? Who is able to make war with him?"*

This evil dictator will be so effective in his methods that he will even create a system of commerce that he and his kingdom will be able to control. This system will mandate that anyone who wants to buy or sell anything must be connected and a willing member of his system. Every citizen will then be required to be "marked" in order to utilize the system to buy or sell. The Bible seems to indicate two or even three separate "marks" may be utilized, and which mark a person receives will be dictated by class or their position in society.

Our Main Passage

Let's look more closely at the first part of our central passage of our study in Scripture. In Revelation 13 verses 16-17. It reads, *"And he causeth all, both small and great, rich and poor, free and bond, to receive a mark in their right hand, or in their foreheads: 17 And that no man might buy or sell, save he that had the mark, or the name of the beast, or the number of his name." (KJV)*

Martin W Sondermann

I wonder if you caught that?

This "mark of the beast" that so many talk about, and that so many assume will be 6-6-6, isn't a single mark at all. The Scriptures states there in verse 17 that *"no man might buy or sell, save he that had the mark, OR the name of the beast, OR the number of his name."*

Do you see that?

A person will not be able to buy or sell unless they have the mark, OR unless they have the name of the beast, OR, unless they have the number of his name. I don't know about you, but a mark, a number, and a name are at least three different things.

"Well, wait a second," you might say. "That's just the translation or something."

Actually, it's not just this translation. Let me give you a few other word-for-word translations. In the NASB it reads, *"And he provides that no one will be able to buy or to sell,*

Mark(s) of the Beast

except the one who has the mark, either the name of the beast or the number of his name."

"See," you might say. "Right there in the NASB it says, "no one will be able to buy or to sell, except the one who has the mark, either the name of the beast or the number. So that's just two different kind of markings isn't it?"

Great point and you might be right. There may just be two markings, but I also want to point out something about the translation. Do you see the word "either" in this verse? That word was added by the translator in hopes that it would bring clarity to the verse. Let's read that verse with the translator insert removed. *"And that no one will be able to buy or to sell, except the one who has the mark, the name of the beast or the number of his name."* This seems to me to still be saying that there will be at least two markings, and maybe even three!

Let's look at other word-for-word translations. The Amplified Bible reads, *"And that no one will be able to buy or sell, except the one who has the mark, either the name of the beast or the number of his name."* Again, remove the additional "either" which was added by the translator, and you see two or three markings. The New King James says it this way; *"And that no one may buy or sell except one who has the mark or the name of the beast, or the number of his name."* If you read it plainly this translation displays three distinct types of this mark. However, it must be noted that a footnote in the NKJ Bible tells us that a majority of the original texts and fragments of Scripture that we have, actually omit the "or" following the word mark. So, with that removed it would read, *"and that no one may buy or sell except one who has the mark the name of the beast, or the number of his name."* To me it doesn't seem to fit when translated this way, but even if that were the correct translation it still appears as if there could be three distinct markings, but at the very least two are still present.

The Holman Christian Standard Bible actually adds a colon after the word mark so as to make sense of it. *"So that no one can buy or sell unless he has the mark: the beast's name or the number of his name."* Again, it still doesn't seem to flow all that well, but at the very least there are still two markings to deal with, the beast's name or the number of his name.

Mark(s) of the Beast

Young's literal translation reads this way, *"and that no one may be able to buy, or to sell, except he who is having the mark, or the name of the beast, or the number of his name."* Darby's English translation reads; *"and that no one should be able to buy or sell save he that had the mark, the name of the beast, or the number of its name."* Also, Noah Webster's translation was similar, *"And that no man might buy or sell, save him that had the mark, or the name of the beast, or the number of his name."*

Now, I am no Greek expert, and I do not claim to be. We've already established this. But, over the years much smarter men than me have translated this verse with at least two or, at the most, three distinct markings. These markings are not just the familiar 6-6-6, or what is known as the number of the beast.

From my study I have come to an understanding that there is certainly more than one "mark". I haven't been convinced that there are three distinct marks, but I am convinced that there will be at least two. If it be "two marks" I believe then the proper understanding would be that the "mark" is a general description of what will be placed on individuals, but this "mark" would be given in two forms; the "name" and the "number". However, as the

Martin W Sondermann

Bible seems to indicate, there will be some kind of association between the "number" and the "name". What I mean by that is the name of the beast will somehow calculate out to the number of the beast. I think Scripture is clear on that. How that will be accomplished is anyone's guess. I know some probably think they have the answer, but I just can't say that for myself. Besides I have never been very good at math.

Now, could I be wrong about this? Sure, I could be wrong, I guess. But at least I would be in great company. But, in looking at this verse closely I believe something is there that warrants further inspection, and I believe it is a reasonable response to believe there will be more than one kind of marking.

God Marks His People

Something else to think about is that as I mentioned earlier the Anti-Christ, False-Prophet, and Satan himself will be committing the ultimate counterfeit during the tribulation. I think we are also going to see Satan use this same kind of counterfeiting when it comes to the multiple markings on the people of the earth during the tribulation. Let me explain.

Mark(s) of the Beast

In the book of Ezekiel chapter 9 we see a story about the wickedness among God's people in the Temple located in Jerusalem. Ezekiel has a vision, and in it he hears God's booming voice in the last part of verse 1 calling for, *"them that have charge over the city to draw near, even every man with his destroying weapon in his hand." (KJV)* It goes on to state in verse 2, *"And, behold six men came from the way of the higher gate, which lieth toward the north, and every man a slaughter weapon in his hand; and one man among them was clothed with linen, with a writer's inkhorn by his side: and they went in, and stood beside the brazen altar.*

Something interesting to note here is that these six "men" here in this passage are most likely angels arriving from "the way of the higher gate". Angels are often described in Scripture in this way because of their appearance. Many Biblical scholars agree from the total description in this passage that this group of six "men" are most likely of heavenly origins. In fact, this group appears to be the angelic force that has the assignment or duty of watching over the well-being of Jerusalem. We see this kind of example a few different times in Scripture where good and bad angels have some kind of bond or assignment

Martin W Sondermann

to a group of people or geographical area. In the Book of Daniel chapter 10 we see a demonic spirit attached to Persia, and we also know that Satan himself was somehow associated with the king of Babylon. We also know that Michael the Archangel has a special guardian relationship with the nation Israel. In the same way I believe these angels in Ezekiel were assigned by God to watch over Jerusalem, and the Temple area.

Another powerful picture being painted here is that in verse 3 God calls to the one angel dressed in "linen". Linen garments were worn by the priests in the Temple of God, and this I believe is an angel wearing a priestly garment. Perhaps his duty was to watch over the priests of Israel. But that is only my own speculation. This angel is also the one with the "inkhorn" by his side. Verse 3 reads, *"And the glory of the God of Israel was gone up from the cherub, whereupon he was, to the threshold of the house. And he called to the man clothed with linen, which had the writer's inkhorn by his side;"* Verse 4 then tells us what God says to him, *"And the LORD said unto him, Go through the midst of the city, through the midst of Jerusalem, and set a mark upon the foreheads of the men*

Mark(s) of the Beast

that sigh and that cry for all the abominations that be done in the midst thereof." (KJV)

God is about to bring a brutal judgment upon the people of Jerusalem. But before He allows His judgment to fall upon those in the city, he instructs this angelic priestly figure to take his ink and *"set a mark upon the foreheads of the men that sigh and cry for all the abominations"*. In other words, God is telling him to "mark" all of the men whose hearts are broken like God's heart is broken, and they will be saved from the judgment to come. And, that is what we read happens in the rest of the story. Destruction comes to the wicked, but only those with the "mark" of God on their foreheads are saved.

Something very intriguing in this story is that the word used for "mark" in the Hebrew language is "Tawv". This word is actually the name for the last letter in the Hebrew alphabet. Something to note about the Hebrew alphabet, at least the ancient Hebrew alphabet, is that each of the 22 letters has a symbolic meaning. The letter "Tawv" is in the form of a cross, and its meaning is a sign a monument, or a mark. I personally don't believe it's an accident that God placed a cross on the foreheads of the righteous men of Jerusalem to save them from destruction. I think it was

Martin W Sondermann

simply a testimony of the fact that the Cross was in God's plan from the very beginning, and I think God used the cross or "Tawv" in a way that points people to the redemptive work of Jesus through the saving of these righteous men of Jerusalem centuries before.

In Revelation chapter 7 we see another group of men sealed for safety by God. The word used in the Greek for "sealed" is "sphragizo" which means to stamp. God then places this stamp in these men's foreheads just as seen in Ezekiel chapter 9. Revelation chapter 7 verses 3 and 4 read, *"Saying, Hurt not the earth, neither the sea, nor the trees, till* __*we have sealed the servants of our God in their*__ __*foreheads*__*. 4 And I heard the number of them which were sealed: and there were sealed an hundred and forty and four thousand of all the tribes of the children of Israel."* *(KJV)*

The Bible then goes on to tell us that 12,000 men from 12 different tribes of Israel were sealed. The important thing to note for our study is that we see a second time God has "marked" His people.

In Revelation chapter 14 verse 1, which is part of the 20 verses following our main passage, we see this same group of 144,000 standing on Mount Zion with the Lamb. This time is states that the name of the Father is written in their foreheads, *"And I looked and, lo, a lamb stood on the Mount Sion, and with him an hundred forty and four thousand, having his Father's name written in their foreheads."* *(KJV)*

When you put it all together it appears as if twice and perhaps three times, God places some kind of mark in the forehead of His people. I say this because we see the 144,000 in chapter 7 of Revelation receiving a seal that is equated to a "stamp", but in chapter 14 we see this same group with a mark that is the name of the Father. This could be the same "mark", but if so, why didn't Scripture just say so? God is very specific, and if the seal in chapter 7 was the name of the Father I believe it would have said so as well. But, again, that's just my opinion, and it may or may not be important. At this point, I just don't know.

What I do know is that we have already looked at the passage in Revelation 13 relating to the name, the number, and the mark of the beast being two different marks or even three depending on the language. I think this is nothing more than another satanic counterfeit trying to be like God. After all, in Scripture we see God "marking" His people at least twice and possibly three times. In Ezekiel 9 we see

God marking His men with the "Tawv" or cross, and then in Revelation 7 we see Him using a "seal" or stamp to identify His people. Lastly, in Revelation 14 we see God's people with The Father's name in their foreheads. Again, this could be the same as the "seal" in chapter 7, but it is ambiguous in Scripture so I could see how some would believe it to be two different markings, and some might see three.

But ultimately, I think all of this indicates once again that Satan does all he can to counterfeit the real deal. He is the ultimate deceiver, and during the tribulation his false version of the Trinity will imitate many things of God in an effort to bring a world to its collective knees in an unholy act of worship.

Opinions Don't Stand Alone

One last thing I want to note when it comes to the interpretation I am presenting in this book as it relates to the multiple forms of markings of the Anti-Christ kingdom. This can't just be my own invention or idea. In 2 Peter chapter 1 verses 20 and 21 it reads; *"Knowing this first, that no prophecy of the Scripture is of any private interpretation. 21 For the prophecy came not in old time*

Mark(s) of the Beast

by the will of man but holy men of God spake as t₁
moved by the Holy Ghost." (KJV)

I am not so arrogant to think that somehow, I have gained secret knowledge, and I am certainly not looking to be a contrarian just for the sake of trying to impress, argue, or be different for different sake. No, in fact, in writing this book I am laying my study out for all to see as a way to test this matter. If my interpretation is wrong, then it should be corrected. If it is correct, then I would just ask that you consider it. No matter what results I received I do hope that this study provokes others to study God's Word. I also hope it helps to start a dialogue with other believers in Jesus Christ about the days in which we find ourselves, and the issues that are becoming more relevant as the time of Christ's return draws near.

Martin W Sondermann

Chapter 8

Separate Classes

We Won't Know for Sure—Hopefully

Among believers one of the most intriguing and probably most discussed topics relating to the mark of the beast is what will the mark be? Will it be a chip? Will it be a tattoo? Will it be some other kind of technology?

Now, before we jump too far into this chapter, I want to make something perfectly clear. What the "mark" or "marks" are going to be is pure speculation. I do not believe there is any way right now to know for certain what the mark of beast will be, and if it is multiple kinds of marks, whether or not different technologies will be utilized.

I personally believe different technologies will be used for the mark and/or the name, and the number of the name. I also believe that because there seems to be some kind of difference in these markings, I am going to explain to you my theory that perhaps the type of mark a person will receive during the tribulation might be an indication about which part of society that individual belongs to.

Watch Your Language

To look at the type of marks that might be used by the Anti-Christ's kingdom I think we first need to look closely at the Biblical words used to describe them. Once again Revelation 13:16-17 reads, ***"16 And he causeth all, both small and great, rich and poor, free and bond, to receive a <u>mark</u> in their right hand, or in their foreheads: 17 And that no man might buy or sell, save he that had the <u>mark</u>, or the name of the beast, or the number of his name."*** ***(KJV)***

The word used for "mark" in the Greek is "charagma". According to Strong's it means, *"a scratch or etching, that is, stamp (as a badge of servitude), or sculptured figure (statue): - graven, mark."* The word comes from the Greek root word "charax" which according to Strong's means, *"To sharpen to a point, through the idea of scratching; a stake, that is, (by implication) a palisade or rampart (military mound for circumvallation in a siege): - trench."* Strong's goes on to explain that this word is "akin to the

Greek word "grapho" which means, *"to grave, especially to write; figuratively to describe."*

There are two things when looking at this word closely that jump off the page to me. First, this is some kind of stamp or etching. This would seem to indicate that whatever the "mark" is it is something that is pressed, written, or carved in the skin. I'm not dogmatic about this, but only taking from the definition things that appear interesting.

The second thing that deserves our attention about this word is how much is packed in to the definition. The word used here by the Holy Spirit to describe the mark is extremely profound. When you look at the definition of this word it not only relates to a sculpted figure or statue, but it's also related to a badge of servitude, and a military term "circumvallation" which means to surround. When you understand that the Anti-Christ will be using this mark during a time of military conquest, and during the time of the creation of an image that the world will have to worship (serve), it really is amazing how perfect this word is.

Military

Mark(s) of the Beast

Since my theory is that there might be three, or at least two separate "marks" I want to share with you how I think those marks will be assigned. My theory, and it is only a theory, is that if there are three marks, the "mark" will be utilized to identify military personnel loyal to the Anti-Christ. I believe this because of the fact that this word has military associations, and I also believe the military personnel will be the first to receive a "mark" during the tribulation, which is why I believe it is listed first on the list.

The Elites

As far as the next marking on the list it seems a bit more intimate. The verse goes on to say that no one can buy or sell unless they have the mark, or the "name" of the beast. The word used for "name" is "onoma" in the Greek. This word literally means a name, but it can also be used figuratively. This word signifies authority or character according to Strong's. In other words, the person marked with a name is operating or identifying with the authority and character of the one to which the name belongs.

Onoma also has a couple root words it is associated with. The first is "ginosko". This word is a verb, and it basically means to know in a way that is in-depth and intimate. The second root word is "oniemi" which is also a verb relating to notoriety and gratification. According to Strong's it is defined as; "to derive pleasure or advantage from." When you put all of the understanding of the word "onoma" or "name" it paints a clear picture. Those who receive the "name of the beast" at least appear to be intimate with the beast in some way. These with the "name" will most likely speak on behalf of the beast and have an understanding of what he wants and desires.

I believe those with the "name" will be the elites, and the ruling class. This would make sense because the Anti-Christ will certainly need their support to build his powerful base.

My theory about this is that the Anti-Christ and False-Prophet will build support quickly with many promises of continued riches and ruling power. When the system instituted by the Anti-Christ kingdom commences the ruling class and the elites will need to be placated. This will be done, in my opinion, by massaging their egos through elite access, and a special designation that raises them above the average Joe. They will no doubt be involved in intimate meetings with this evil world leader and be well-versed in his agenda and purpose. Again, this is just my opinion. I mean it's a really good opinion, but an opinion, nonetheless.

The Masses

Lastly, the "number" of the beast will most likely be just that. I personally think this "number" marking will be for the masses in general. The word used here in the Greek is "arithmos", and you might already know, or can guess, that this is where the word arithmetic comes from in our English language. The word is defined by Strong's as, *"a number (as reckoned up): - number:"* It seems pretty straight forward to me. There are also some root words involved that give some interesting things to think about. One of the root words is "airo". It is a verb that has a huge variety of possible meanings. In Strong's the first thing it lists for meaning is "to lift". It goes on to add, *"Accept, advance, and arise."*

Pausing there I think there are some insights to ponder. We know that during the tribulation no one will be able to buy or sell without the mark of the beast. My theory is that the Anti-Christ kingdom will come to the rescue during a time of world-wide crisis. That kingdom will most likely offer food, medicine, supplies, and shelter if needed to those willing to line up and be counted. It will be an answer to the prayers of many answered by a false god. This will be advertised as a way to "raise them up" out of their current situation.

My theory is that at military forces backing the Anti-Christ kingdom will receive a mark first. Then those in powerful positions, the super wealthy, the famous and influential will be next in line. This will most likely correspond with the promotion of the number or mark for the masses. I could foresee celebrity spokesman telling the masses to line up and sign up. Join the club will be the message. Why not? All the rich and famous people are doing it. Don't you want to be like the beautiful people? You want to be part of the cool crowd—don't you? After all, think of your children.

If the Scripture is simply stating that there is one "mark" and it is given in two different forms, i.e. the "name" and the "number", then my theory still holds true. The only difference here is that I believe the elites, the famous, the influential, the super-wealthy, and government officials will be given the "name", and the masses will be given the "number". If this is the scenario, I could see the military masses given the number, but the higher up leadership would receive the name.

In either scenario I believe there will be a distinction between classes of people. It will be a way to elevate the elite as to separate them from the lowly. This will allow the rich and powerful to enjoy, for a season at least, the benefits of serving as makeshift demigods in a counterfeit kingdom with a counterfeit god as its leader.

"Nice story," you say? "But do you have any other Scripture to back this up fella?"

Hey now, there is no need to get testy, but I do indeed have some passages to back up my theory. It starts with the fact that during the tribulation God makes note that when all hell is breaking loose on earth, the rich still seem to be enjoying their luxurious lifestyles. In Revelation 6 verse 6 we see something interesting; *"And I heard a voice in the midst of the four beasts say, A measure of wheat for a penny, and three measures of barley for a penny; and see thou hurt not the oil and the wine." (KJV)*

Martin W Sondermann

This verse directly follows what is known as the "Third Horse". This horse is black, and its rider carries a pair of balances in his hands. We see that during this time period there is going to be a famine, and a lack of everyday food items. When the Bibles states; *"A measure of wheat for a penny, and three measures of barley for a penny"* what it is saying is, "a day's wages for the ingredients for a loaf of bread". Not a day's wages for a loaf of bread, but rather, a day's wages for just the ingredients to make bread. This is testifying of a time of extreme poverty and want by the masses. However, notice something peculiar. The verse states; *"And see thou hurt not the oil and the wine".*

At first glance you might think, "So what?"

But I tell you it's a profound portion of Scripture. Oil and wine are luxury items. These items testify of wealth and abundance. We see in Chapter 6 of Revelation that the poor, and the common man will be longing for sustenance. But, the rich, at least for a season, will still have their luxury items. In my opinion this verse shows us that the rich, the elite, and perhaps those with the "name" will indeed enjoy the benefits for a season.

"Is that all you got?" You ask.

Mark(s) of the Beast

First of all, you don't have to be so cynical. Second, no, it's not the only passage that I believe points to different classes of people receiving different kinds of "marks". In fact, it was right under your nose the entire time we looked at verses 16 and 17 in Revelation 13. *"16 And he causeth all, both small and great, rich and poor, free and bond, to receive a mark in their right hand, or in their foreheads: 17 And that no man might buy or sell, save he that had the mark, or the name of the beast, or the number of his name." (KJV)*

Do you see it now?

No?

Well, let me explain.

The Bible says "he", meaning the Anti-Christ, *"causes all, both small and great, rich and poor, free and bond, to receive a mark"*. I think it's profound and meaningful that it states, **"he causes both"** and then lists three groups categorized by two classifications each. I mean why would it say "both" if there were so many things listed?

My opinion is that God did this to show us there will be two main categories of people during the tribulation, and I believe all three descriptions break those two groups into

Martin W Sondermann

categories. The "great" are also the "rich" and the "free". The "small" are also the "poor" and "bond". For those that don't know, bond is simply a slave or servant. When you assemble it all with the fact that the Bible states there will be a marking called a "name" and one called the "number" I don't think it's a far leap to determine how those different markings will be administered. One to the rich and powerful, and one to the masses. Even if there are three marks, they will be separated by one to the elites, and the other two for the military and masses. After all, the military are "servants."

Again, and I know you are tired of hearing me say it, but this is just my opinion. But I didn't just grab this opinion out of the sky. I have formulated what I believe through the careful study of God's Word, and prayerful consideration. I honestly believe there are going to be two, and maybe three different kinds of markings. From my study, and what I shared with you I hope you can see how arrived at this.

Chapter 9

Technologies of the Marks

What Will It Be?

During the tribulation period many in the world will line up willingly to receive the marks of the beast. Whether that is a single mark, two marks, or even three, the fact remains that some form of technology will have to be utilized. Once again I must say for the record that I am not saying that any of the companies or technologies written about in this chapter will have anything to do with this coming system of buying or selling under the Anti-Christ's reign, but what I am saying is that I could see how similar things could be used.

After all, somebody's technology will be utilized.

The Barcode

One of the most commonly held beliefs about the Mark of the Beast is that it will be a Barcode or Universal

Product Code (UPC). I doubt there are any people reading this book that don't know what a Barcode is, or at the very least, if they don't recognize the name, they likely would recognize the image of lines and numbers that are now present on nearly every item sold in retail stores and online. No doubt like the one on the back of this book.

The Barcode is a marking that consists of lines and numbers. It is a mark that can be read by optical devices and each group of lines and numbers represent data that describes and identifies the item. The Barcode was first used in a professional environment in the 1970's. National Cash Register, a company that provided point of sale systems for retailers, placed Barcodes on grocery items in a supermarket in Troy, Ohio in 1974, and the rest is history. However, the journey from concept to retail stores didn't begin in the 1970's. It didn't even start in the 60's or even the 50's. No, the interesting fact about the Barcode is that it has its roots in the year 1948.

1948

For Biblical Scholars, and for anyone who studies Biblical prophecy, the year 1948 is significant. It is after all; the year Israel once again became an official nation fulfilling Biblical prophecy. It was May 14, 1948 in Tel

Mark(s) of the Beast

Aviv, Israel that Chairman David Ben-Gurion proclaimed the State of Israel. This was after over 1,900 years of the Jewish people being out of The Land and scattered among the nations. Many Biblical Scholars point to this as a key element of end times prophecy because much of what must occur, must happen in the nation of Israel after many Jewish people return from the four corners of the globe. This has happened dramatically over the decades and is another key sign that we are living in the days just before the return of Jesus Christ. But you guessed it, that's another amazing study for another day.

As for the year 1948 I am not saying there is anything overly spiritual going on, but for the idea of the Barcode to happen in that same year seems, perhaps, a little more than a coincidence. As for the connection, it goes like this. The creator of the Barcode and its system is a man named Joe Woodland. Mr. Woodland was born in 1921, and it must be noted that he himself was Jewish. As far as his inspiration to create the Barcode it came after talking with a supermarket employee that needed a way to speed up check out times. Woodland thought the idea was so good that he decided to drop out of graduate school to begin pursuing the Barcode invention. This happened in the winter of

1948. And, although he didn't arrive at a working invention until early 1949, I still argue that the connection to 1948 means something.

Barcode technology came from Woodland's understanding of Morse code which he learned in the Scouts. Now, although Woodland had the idea, there was still no way to read the code itself. He tried various electronic devises of the time, but Woodland was so advanced with his idea that it took another two decades before a computer device adequate enough to read his code would be invented. The "laser" came around in the 1960's, and versions of Woodland's Barcode were mostly round, and not easy to reproduce. A group of people got together in an effort make a universal mark that would be easier to produce and read. Long story short, and after IBM got involved, a man named George Laurer led the charge in creating a more readable Barcode. Laurer was successful of course, and the rest is history.

That 6-6-6 Connection

One of the reasons there is mild controversy over the 12-digit Universal Product Code (UPC), also known as the Barcode, is the fact that it "marks" nearly everything we buy or sell. Not only that, but the pattern of lines which represent the number "six" also appear at the beginning, in the middle, and at the end of every Barcode. In other words, each set of lines represent a number, and the lines that represent the number six begin, divide, and end every single Barcode. And, while I don't believe there was anything sinister intended by its creator, I do think this to be one heck of a coincidence.

When asked about this "coincidence" the UPC creator reportedly admitted that the number six and the separation lines resemble each other, but he also stated, *"There is nothing sinister about this nor does it have anything to do with the Bible's mark of the beast... It is simply a coincidence."*[ix]

Coincidence or not, and even though its creators may have not had any ulterior motives, there is always the possibility that a version of the Barcode could be used by the Anti-Christ. The technology is not evil, and no one is claiming that it is. As mentioned previously, the Anti-Christ will use someone's invention, and someone's technology. The Barcode or UPC is a very inexpensive and easy way to mark things, and in its current state could number items up to 999,999,999,999. That is certainly enough to number the population of the world which during the tribulation would be most likely under six billion. But there is the funny issue of numbering people with existing product numbers. Because millions of Barcodes are currently in use today, if the Anti-Christ does use this system it will probably have to be some kind of variation of numbers. Also, it would be easy enough to place Barcodes on individuals and tie them into a database.

UID

One other form of identification similar to the UPC Barcode that must be noted is the UID program. This stands for Unique Identification Program, and it's a required tracking system for anyone doing business with the United States military, and the military uses the system to track all of its assets.

Will UPC or UID be used as the "number of the beast"? Is either going to be one of the marks?

Who knows? But what we do know is that whatever is coming will at least be similar.

Application

When it comes to placing a mark, whether it's the Barcode or another kind of mark, there will need to be a way to apply such a mark. Tattooing seems to be an option, and there are quick and easy ways to do that these days.

Mark(s) of the Beast

Not only that, but if you look around at society people have become very fond of getting inked up for various reasons. Whether it's sports figures, actors, singers, or just the average Joe or Jane, tattoos have become very popular. I wonder if Satan didn't have a hand in this cultural shift as of the last few decades.

Inked Up Generation

Now, before I explain my understanding let me say this; I do not think you are going to Hell if you have a tattoo. I also don't believe you have received the mark of the beast or that you can't be a Christian and have a tattoo. That's between you and God and my opinion doesn't matter. I personally have decided not to get tattoos simply because of a Scripture I read years ago. Again, before you put the book down, I am not judging anyone. This was my personal conviction, and there is personal meaning for me. I don't put that on anyone else. Whatever God has said to you about tattoos is between you and Him. After all, the verses before this one I am about to share talk about not rounding the corners of your hair or beard. I have never had any conviction about that, in fact, I have only grown a full beard three times in my whole life. So please, relax if you have tattoos. No one is judging you here.

Martin W Sondermann

The verse I am talking about is found in the book of Leviticus, and it was a command given to the Jewish people. Leviticus chapter 19 verse 28 says, *"Ye shall not make any cuttings in your flesh for the dead, nor print any marks upon you: I am the LORD." (KJV)* The New King James actually translates it this way, *"You shall not make any cuttings in your flesh for the dead, nor tattoo any marks on you: I am the LORD."*

When I read this verse, I can't help but think that it was not just instructing the Jews of that day. I believe, like so many versus in the Bible, it was also reaching across the corridor of time to a generation centuries in the future. We know that during the Tribulation God is going to be dealing with the Jewish people corporately. It is after all, the time we know as Daniel's 70th Week, or the time of Jacob's trouble. Right now, in this time-period, we see that tattoos have become very popular, and I wonder if it isn't the enemy's way to condition a future generation to receive his satanic tattoo, otherwise known as the Mark of the Beast.

Electronic Tattoos

Speaking of tattoos did you know that several companies and have already patented electronic tattoos? However, what is being called a tattoo is really just an electronic sticker of sorts. But, to be fair, it is unlike any sticker you have ever heard of. These stickers, at least some of them, can interact with the body, and the mind. They can store all kinds of information, and even relay it to distant computers. Imagine if an advanced version of these electronic tattoos could be implemented in mass one day and attached to a global network. One of the biggest drawbacks to this kind of technology is that the stickers don't last long, but give them time, and they will find a way to make it permanent.

RFID

One of the permanent methods of marking human beings is in current use in humans and animals. It is called RFID or Radio Frequency Identification, and it was invented by a man named Harry Stockman. Oh, by the way, he invented RFID in 1948. Another coincidence, I guess.

In his scholarly work *"Communication by Means of Reflected Power"* published in Proceedings of the IRE, pp1196-1204, October 1948[x], Stockman explains his findings, *"Point-to-point communication, with the carrier power generated at the receiving end and the transmitter replaced by a modulated reflector, represents a transmission system which possesses new and different characteristics. Radio, light, or sound waves (essentially microwaves, infrared, and ultrasonic waves) may be used for the transmission under approximate conditions of specular reflection."*

That last term there is very curios to me. Especially when I read the language of the definition remembering that the name Lucifer means "light bearer" or "bringing light". Remember it was Lucifer (Satan) that wanted to be like the Most High God. It was Lucifer that decided to rebel, and it will be Lucifer behind every single marking in the tribulation period.

In its current capacity RFID system, is an identification method. It stores and then retrieves data as needed from something called an RFID tag. This "tag" can be inserted into animals or people as a way to track, identify, or store medical or other information as needed. They can also be used on packages to track them, vehicles, clothing, keys so you don't lose them, medicine, and a variety of other everyday uses.

RFID tags can be stickers, or as physically insert-able devices as small as a grain of rice. Each tag contains an integrated circuit with storage capacity, an antenna of

Mark(s) of the Beast

various sizes to broadcast and receive data and communication, and some form of casing.

Active RFID tags, unlike passive tags, also require a power source such as a battery. They also give off a "beacon" about every 5 seconds in an effort to send out its information and can be read usually from a distance of about up to the length of a football field. But that technology is getting better, and relays and other options can boost the signal.

RFID tags in their current form do have limitations to be used as a mark of the beast. The biggest problem is they don't do well in metal or water. Also, active RFID require new batteries when old ones run out. Until a method to have the body power them, or some kind of recharging capability is widely available the technology is limited for massive identification of human beings, at least when it comes to efficient tracking. The passive tag could be used right now to mark people, and in fact it is currently in use with humans and animals. It just requires outside power from some kind of reader device. And, again, I am not saying if you have one of these implants that you have taken the mark of the beast. In a future chapter we are going to find that every single person that <u>takes</u> (not

Martin W Sondermann

forced), the mark of the beast will do so willingly, will know what they are doing, and will give their worship to the Anti-Christ willingly.

If while reading this, you begin to think that widespread RFID use isn't feasible I want you think about this. In the summer of 2017, a Wisconsin based Technology Company named Three Square Market began giving its employees the option of being implanted with a passive RFID chip. This would allow those implanted to swipe into the building, to pay for food items at the company's cafeteria, and other security-based procedures. Although the implant was not mandatory 50 of the 80 employees had already lined up to be chipped despite the fact that they could be tracked anywhere within the company, and I guess that means even the bathroom. Just think about that.

Will RFID implants be one of the marks? Will a form of this technology be used in the Tribulation? I really don't know if it will be. Just consider the fact that our cell phones are already more intrusive and a better way to track people. Their weakness, as it relates to the mark of the beast, is that they (phones) are not implanted, and can be disposed of. But what if cell phones and RFID tags were somehow connected? Or what if cell phones and some other implantable technology were to merge into one device?

Your Stupid Smartphone

Cell phones, they are aptly named if you ask me. Although cell is short for cellular, I think cell is more appropriate. These phones, in essence, have created our own little free-roaming prison cells. We can't escape its dominion, and many of us panic if we lose it or forget it at home. In a way, we have all given up our freedom for convenience, and because most of us are addicted to them, it has become an accepted practice in society. I also firmly believe that even if the cell phone isn't involved in the mark of the beast it has certainly been used to condition all of us. Think about it, during the tribulation people will get a mark in their right hands or in their foreheads. We have become very comfortable using a device in our hands that is placed against our heads. We have become comfortable giving up our privacy and freedom and allowing companies and our own government to monitor us day and night, all for the sake of stupid games, foolish apps, and constant distractions. Before you ask, yes, I use one. I won't try to justify it or make excuses. I have been conditioned just like anyone else, but I have learned to be cautious, and not rely solely on such a device for critical matters.

Combine all of the technology I am speaking of in this chapter, with what was written in earlier chapters, along with social media like Facebook, Twitter, and the like, and you have a world-wide monitoring system that knows nearly everything about everyone. Then, implant everyone on the planet, and you have instant full-time access to monitoring every person whether they are logged on or not. If they are walking in the streets 5G has them covered. If they are out in the Mountains the satellite internet keeps them connected. It could all be done through the internet itself as the receiver for every RFID tag, implanted chip, electronic tattoo, or whatever is used as the mark, the name, or the number.

In fact, did you know that in 2016 the European Union proposed a government identification number be issued to anyone using the internet? It would keep track of everything someone did online including shopping, surfing websites, downloading files, and every comment made. It made me think a push for a world-wide identifier can't be far behind.

Mark(s) of the Beast

Sore Losers

Maybe during the tribulation, the masses receive the "number" which is a Barcode, and maybe the military receive an implant which leaves a "mark". Maybe the elites receive some form of trendy electronic tattoo with the "name" of the beast in form of a logo of sorts. Who really knows? I do believe that there seems to be some kind of similarity in all three (or two) markings. Because in Revelation 16 verse 2 we read, *"So the first went and poured out his bowl upon the earth, and a foul and loathsome sore came upon the men who had the mark of the beast and those who worshiped his image" (NKJ)*

We see here that those who receive the "mark" and those who worship the beast will also receive a "foul and loathsome sore". Each one will receive the same punishment for their actions. Look closer, *"a foul and loathsome sore came upon the men <u>who had the mark</u> of the beast and <u>those who worshiped his image.</u>"*

Could this passage be saying that a sore will come upon them which receive the mark, and who also worship the image of the beast? Meaning, they would have to be willing participants. That would then open the question of whether

Martin W Sondermann

or not someone could be forced to receive the mark of the beast, and still be saved during the tribulation.

If you are like me, you have always learned that no one who receives the mark of the beast during the tribulation will be able to be saved. However, Scripture seems to have a prerequisite for those who seal their own fate by the taking a mark and find themselves destined for Hell.

If you read Revelation chapter 14 verses 9 through 11 you see something that I believe to be fascinating, *"And the third angel followed them, saying with a loud voice, If any man worship the beast and his image, and receive his mark in his forehead, or in his hand, 10 The same shall drink of the wine of the wrath of God, which is poured out without mixture into the cup of his indignation; and he shall be tormented with fire and brimstone in the presence of the holy angels, and in the presence of the Lamb: 11 And the smoke of their torment ascendeth up for ever and ever: and they have no rest day nor night, who worship the beast and his image, and whosoever receiveth the mark of his name." (KJV)*

If you look at this passage, we see several interesting things, but I want to just focus on two. First, there seems to be delineation between at least two different kinds of marks

Mark(s) of the Beast

in this passage. In verses 9 and 10 we see that, *"if any man worship the beast and his image, and receive his mark in his forehead, or in his hand,"* that man will *"drink of the wine of the wrath of God,"* and he will also, *"be tormented with fire and brimstone."* Then in verse 11 we see a further description of those that, *"receiveth the mark of his name."* Now, again, maybe the mark is just described as a name or even a number. Or, maybe there are two or even three different kinds of marks like I have discussed. No matter what that turns out to be, the destiny of those who receive it, and worship the beast is the same. They will face God's wrath, and eternal separation and torment in a real place called Hell.

In Revelation chapter 15 verses 1 and 2 we read another very curious description. This time we see not only the mark being mentioned, but also the *"number of his name."* Verse 1 starts, *"And I saw another sign in heaven, great and marvelous, seven angels having the seven last plagues; for in them is filled up the wrath of God. 2 And I saw as it were a sea of glass mingled with fire: and them that had gotten the victory over the beast, and over his image, and over his mark, and over the number of his*

Martin W Sondermann

name, stand on the sea of glass, having the harps of God." (KJV)

The Willing

These two verses are no doubt speaking about those men and women during the tribulation who refused to bow to the image, worship the beast, or receive his mark or his number. But I have always wondered what would happen to someone during those days if they were <u>forcibly</u> given the mark against their own will. Most who refuse will be killed of course, but what if there are some who are given a mark by force? Would they also suffer the wrath of God, and eternal judgment in Hell?

In passages such as Revelation 16 verse 2, 19 verse 20, and chapter 20 verse 4, we see that there is something that lines up with the other verses in Revelation we have looked at concerning the mark of the beast. In every instance, without exception, it tells us that people are going to "receive" the mark. Even though in one of our main verses found in chapter 13 verse 17 we see that the Anti-Christ will "causeth" all" to receive a mark, and even though there seems to be some kind of demand for people to receive it, nowhere does it indicate that they are forced to do so. Instead it proclaims that people will "receive" the mark.

Mark(s) of the Beast

The word used there for "receive" in the Greek language is "lamano". This word, according to Strong's means, *"to take, in very many applications, literally and figuratively, probably objective or active, to get hold of."* Strong's also notes that the author didn't use the Greek word "dechomai" which is more passive, nor was the word "aihreomai" used which means to be forced to do so. Strong's Concordance states it this way, *"whereas [dechomai] is rather subjective or passive, to have offered to one; while [aihreomai] is more violent, to seize or remove."*

In other words, what is being said here is that people will actively and willingly receive the mark of the beast, or the name, or the number of the name. They will not be forced, nor will it be a passive gesture. However, that doesn't mean that the act of forcing the mark upon some won't happen. I think in those cases if a mark is forced upon a person, and yet they still refuse worship of the beast, they will not be automatically sent to Hell. If that person is someone who puts their faith in Jesus Christ and they are forced to get the mark, but then does not worship the beast nor do they use the privilege of the mark, I just cannot see God sending that person to Hell.

Martin W Sondermann

"Well, do you have Scripture for that theory?" You might ask.

Actually, I do, but most of it is going to sound familiar. In Revelation 14 verses 9 and 10 we read; *"And the third angel followed them, saying with a loud voice, If any man worship the beast and his image, and receive his mark in his forehead, or in his hand, 10 The same shall drink of the wind of the wrath of God, which is poured out without mixture into the cup of his indignation; and he shall be tormented with fire and brimstone in the presence of the holy angels, and in the presence of the Lamb:" (KJV)*

Here we see the connection between receiving the mark and the act of worship. It seems to be a package deal. In fact, when you look at key mentions of the mark of the beast itself in Revelation you see the worship of the beast is linked with the mark of the beast. In verse 11 of chapter 14 we read, *"They have no rest day or night, who worship the beast and his image, and whosoever receiveth the mark of his name."* In Revelation 16 verse 2 it says, *"And there fell a noisome and grievous sore upon the men which had the mark of the beast and them which worshiped his image."* In Revelation 19 verse 20 where it speaks about the judgment of the Anti-Christ and false-prophet they are

Mark(s) of the Beast

joined by those, *"that had received the mark of the beast, and them that worshiped his image."*

This is one of those issues that seem like something that shouldn't be argued over or debated, and I tend to agree. But for those living during the tribulation this will indeed matter. I pray that if a believer is forced to receive the mark, and they do not worship the beast, that there will indeed be a way for them to enter the Kingdom of God. I pray that God will comfort them, and that they will be strong enough not to bow to the pressure, and not to bend the knee.

I am not God, and God's ways are not our ways, but I want to believe that if a follower of Jesus Christ is marked by force, meaning he or she didn't want it, didn't ask for it, and never uses it, that God will indeed allow them to enter into His Kingdom. In Revelation 13 verse 8 we see that many of those on the earth during the time of the Anti-Christ are going to worship him. We also read that there is a group of people sealed from the very foundation of the world. I do not think any of them will be lost. Verse 8 states; *"And all that dwell on the earth shall worship him, whose names are not written in the book of life of the Lamb slain from the foundation of the world."*

Martin W Sondermann

God will not lose a single one that belongs to Him!

Chapter 10

World-Wide Economy

Grandpa's Generation

I remember sitting at a kitchen table with my grandfather in 2005 having a conversation about global economic conditions, and the future. He was an honest man, a hardworking man, and was very good at managing his money. He would occasionally give me advice and share his opinions on the condition of the world and finances. He was an outspoken man. I remember more than a few times where he wrote letters to the local newspapers concerning different political issues. He was well informed and watched news and read the newspapers on a regular basis. He wasn't a person that lived under a rock. Nor was he a person ignorant of the world around him. In fact, I would say my grandfather was one of the most informed people of his generation.

But during our conversation I brought up the fact that everything seemed to be going the way of plastic payment. I explained that most people my age, and especially younger, weren't carrying cash much anymore, and that debit cards had become the norm. I remember telling my grandfather that it wouldn't be long before most people no longer use cash. I thought he would agree with me, but instead he insisted that there was no way people would allow that. Which was true for his generation.

My grandpa was born in 1934. He grew up in a time much different than ours. He was a child during World War II and born during the great depression. He had been taught to be a man of his word, and he practiced saving, not going into debt, and paying cash for items he purchased. Plastic money that somehow processed electronic dollars probably could have never been imagined by him, or most of his peers for that matter. In fact, if you think about the technology gap that exists since the advent of the internet, super computers, smart phones, and banking technologies, there has probably never been a larger generational gap in history, at least as it related to technology. But the gap doesn't just end with my grandfather's generation.

The Growing Gap

That generational technology gap now exists between someone born in the 1990's, and someone born in the first decade of the 2000's. Technology is moving so fast that it has caused exponential advancements, and if a person doesn't keep up almost on a daily basis, they will begin to lag behind quickly. Also, there is such a massive amount of new and advancing technology that it is impossible to keep up with every area. It is almost as if all of us need to choose a specialized section of technology if we even want to stay informed.

During our conversation I began to explain to my grandpa about my generation, and how many of us were using debit cards, not cash. He was almost in disbelief that society was heading that direction. I remember he had a hard time wrapping his head around why people would move away from cash. I don't remember the entire conversation, but his general opinion was that if you had cash you had the power in your hands to control your finances. However, if it was an electronic system then what did you really have? He told me that it was then controlled by those with the computers, and asked me if an error happens with a computer how will you prove the money was there? Other questions he posed were; What happens if someone gets into the computers and steal the money? What happens if someone gets access to your accounts electronically? I knew he had great points, but it also opened my eyes to how fast things were moving, and how the conditioning of generations born in the latter part of the 20th century, and continuing on into the 21st, had been so different than my grandfather's generation.

Fast forward to current time, and it is remarkable how much more has happened to advance a cashless society. In the last fifteen years alone technology in the areas of a cashless society, financial payment processing, banking and finance laws, digital currencies, and security and fraud measures have grown at such a rate that I believe you would be hard pressed to find a handful of people who understand it all, or even a majority of it.

The other day at the supermarket I paid for my groceries with a debit card. This was the kind that now how's a "chip" inserted inside of it. Instead of swiping it I had to push the card into the reading device and wait for "approval" of my own money. After a wait of ten seconds or so, a message read, "Approved, please remove your card."

Bag of Chips

Most people have seen a change of their credit and debit cards in recent months and years. Banks and credit card companies in the United States have been sending out new cards to all of its customers. These "chips" inserted into debit cards, and now part of nearly financial card in the U.S., but I wonder if most customers really know what the addition of this chip even means, or if they even care for that matter.

It's called an EMV chip, and that stands for Europay, MasterCard, and Visa. It is a new "global standard" for credit cards. Much of the world has been using these chip embedded cards for a while, and now the United States is fully on board. We are told that these "chips" are another security measure. We are told it is another layer that makes fraudulent use of our cards more difficult for thieves. The old conventional debit cards used a magnetic stripe where all your information can be found electronically. But the new card doesn't keep the information on board. Instead, this chip speaks to a computer somewhere through an encrypted signal that is read through the store's equipment. It then creates a unique identification for every purchase in an effort to make sure you are who you say you are. It's actually far more secure when the pin is utilized with the card as well, and although most of Europe and other regions require it the United States has been slow in utilized the dual method. I am still not certain how without a pin number required that any financial institution can know it's you using your card. However, maybe they use some kind of algorithm to determine if it fits within your "normal behavior".

I have been reading a lot lately about how everything we do online, including banking transactions, are tracked online, and how each of us is building our own personal algorithm that tells anyone with access what kind of person we are, normal behaviors, interests, and many other unique personality traits. This is done for many reasons such as a way to know what you are interested in so advertisements can be tailored specifically for you. This information can also be used by law enforcement to make sure you aren't searching things related to illegal activities. These kinds of algorithm methods can be so accurate that I have even heard they will be used to stop crimes before they happen just by seeing certain predictive patterns in a person's algorithm. If you think this sounds too futuristic or just too crazy to be true, well, think again. A small amount of research on your own will find that many governments are already experimenting with these kinds of programs and have been for some time now.

In researching this new chip myself, I honestly don't know for sure how this chip knows if it's the proper user or not. I mean what would stop someone from stealing a card, and going to a store to purchase something? It actually seems less secure to me without a pin number because most of the time no one asks for identification when you insert your chip enabled card. It usually does a few things, and then says approved. It would seem to me without the pin there is a bigger risk. Also, there are cards that use RFID tags to just pass in front of scanners to pay for items. They claim to be secure as well, but just give someone the time and they will invent a device that can somehow intercept the signal. Of course, that device already exists.

The Crypt Keeper

We are also seeing a focus put on payment methods via our smartphones. Applications such as Android Pay, or Google Wallet are becoming more-and-more common. Every one of these has its own security risks and issues as well, but the convenience can't be denied. Another thing that has happened in recent years is that a global digital currency has been injected into the mix. Maybe you have heard of Bitcoin? If not, come out from underneath the rock you are living. Just know that it's a digital payment system built as a cryptocurrency.

Martin W Sondermann

Huh? You might ask, a crypto what?

Well, it's a cryptocurrency, and that is defined by the online Oxford dictionary[xi] as; *"A digital currency in which encryption techniques are used to regulate the generation of units of currency and verify the transfer of funds, operating independently of a central bank."*

Bitcoin is the largest and best known of these so-called cryptocurrencies. Here's where it gets really interesting. Bitcoin's inventor is a man named Satoshi Nakamoto. But Mr. Nakamoto probably isn't a real person. Or, at the very least, that isn't his or her real name. In fact, no one knows who invented Bitcoin, but it seems to derive from Japan. Also, it must be noted that the name Nakamoto in Japanese can mean, "central origin". Probably just a coincidence though.

The Bitcoin system works through transactions with no banks, and no one to get in between the buyer and seller. It also doesn't require any identification and costs nothing per transaction. They are not tied to any government or backed by any financial institution. You obtain these Bitcoins through things called Bitcoin Exchanges. These allow people to buy and sell bitcoins with currencies from all over the world. People also "mine" bitcoins through various complex mathematical puzzles. Winners of these puzzles receive Bitcoins, and that is also how new Bitcoins are formed. It almost sounds like we are living in a video game.

It seems to me that one day a centralized system will be officially created, or something like Bitcoin will be adapted to the main stream. It will no doubt utilize many of the technologies currently involved in financial transactions and will likely roll them all into one kind of payment method. After all, we know that during the tribulation this will happen, and again, I am not saying any of these companies named in this chapter will be involved. But we know that the Anti-Christ will have to use someone's technology.

It seems to me we are seeing the building blocks of a global standard of financial transaction rules and regulations merging together to become a single system sometime in the near future.

Be Ready

Looking around the world today it seems pretty obvious to me as a Christian that we are living in the last of the very last days before the return of Jesus Christ. The things predicted in the Bible pertaining to the days leading up to His return seem to be forming right in front of our very eyes.

I wonder, are you ready?

Chapter 11

Why Does it Even Matter?

Maybe your reading this book, and you are thinking to yourself, "Well, okay, thanks for the information so far, but I'm a Christian, and I can't understand why any of this matters to me. After all, if you're right about the Rapture of the Church, then I won't be here, and none of this matters. Does it?"

Well, to you I would answer by saying I believe this matters in a big way for any of us who have put our faith in Jesus Christ. In fact, I am so convinced of that fact that I am going to give you four reasons I believe Christians should be aware of what's coming, and why we should be concerned with the mark of the beast and everything that goes along with it.

First, Study

Study the Word of God because we are commanded to do so. In 2 Timothy chapter 2 verse 15 we are instructed to, ***"Study to shew thyself approved unto God, a workman that needeth not to be ashamed, rightly dividing the word of truth." (KJV)*** God has commanded you and I to study

His Word. Under the inspiration of the Holy Spirit Paul the apostle tells us that we are to study to show ourselves approved unto God. The Bible also tells us that this same Bible we study is "God breathed". In 2 Timothy chapter 3 verse 16 we read, ***"All scripture is given by <u>inspiration</u> of God, and is profitable for doctrine, for reproof, for correction, for instruction in righteousness:" (KJV)***

That word "inspiration" means to breathe. It was God Himself that breathed life into Adam, and it was God Himself who breathed life into His Holy Word.

"But not everything you have printed in this book is the Word of God, so your argument seems a little flimsy," you might say.

Well, I agree that the areas of technology, and the conditions of the world aren't the Word of God, but I do believe it helps us, at the very least, recognize the times in which we live. After all, it was Jesus Himself while answering the Pharisees said the following in Matthew chapter 16 verses 1 through 3; ***"The Pharisees also with the Sadducees came, and tempting desired him that he would shew them a sign from heaven. 2 He answered and***

Mark(s) of the Beast

said unto them, when it is evening, ye say, It will be fair weather: for the sky is red. 3 And in the morning, It will be foul weather today: for the sky is red and lowering. O ye hypocrites, ye can discern the face of the sky; but can ye not discern the signs of the times? (KJV)

Jesus was rebuking the Pharisees and Sadducees for not understanding the times in relationship to His first coming. These men were the ones who should have been able to see, but something had blinded them. They had gotten off-track somewhere along the line, and now these same men who should have been the guardians of the truth, these same men who prided themselves in their rituals and traditions, the very same men who proudly and loudly prayed for the Messiah to come, were the very men who couldn't see Him even when He stood before them on the streets of Israel.

May this be a powerful lesson to all of us. Let us not get so consumed with our own opinions, and our own understandings of doctrine, that we are not open to the Lord's correction and counsel. I pray that all of us will not be those who are caught blindly by the second coming of our Lord. May we all understand the times in which we live and may we all recognize the signs of His soon return.

Martin W Sondermann

In the same chapter in verse 6 Jesus goes on to warn his disciples to, *"beware of the leaven of the Pharisees and of the Sadducees."* Of course, like us, the disciples started analyzing His statement, and directing it toward something they had done, or not done. Jesus then corrects them, and in verses 11 and 12 He explains plainly; *"How is it that ye do not understand that I spake it not to you concerning bread, that ye should beware of the leaven of the Pharisees and of the Sadducees? 12 Then understood they how that he bade them not beware of the leaven of bread, but of the doctrine of the Pharisees and of the Sadducees. (KJV)*

Another great warning for all of us is found within these two verses. May we not get sidetracked by those who seek elevated position over a humble place at the Lord's feet. There are many that proclaim they alone have the truth, or their group is the only one that has it all figured out. Or, even that they have a better truth or a new truth.

Please do not misunderstand what I am saying. I believe whole-heartily that God has placed within His Church excellent leaders, Pastors, and Teachers. But, all of those who serve in such a role should be open to correction and must not use their position to create or propagate any kind

146

of false doctrine. I once heard a Pastor say, "If it's true, it's not new, and if it's new, it's not true." What he meant by this is simply that any new revelation or any new idea in the Church must line-up with the revelation already given to us in the Holy Scriptures. If an idea, doctrine, or revelation goes contrary to the Word of God, then it must be thrown out. It must not be given any place within the Body of Christ. And, I know it is not always simple because there are various interpretations of the very same passages in the Bible. But that's where the original point of "study to show thyself approved unto God" comes into play. We must be a people who study the whole-counsel of God's Word. We must be those that study the Scriptures to know our Lord better, and to better understand what His will and purpose is for our lives, and to equip us in a way to stand against the attack of the enemy, and against our own flesh.

Second, It's Downhill from Here, So Look Up!

The second reason I believe we as Christians should be aware of what is coming is because it helps us understand why things in the world are going the way they are. Not that we shouldn't fight against evil at every turn, but that we might be motivated to continue walking in the light even as the world grows increasingly dark. The enemy is at work, and right now it appears as if he is working overtime. We live in a day-and-age where sin is has become so accepted—and so readily available. It is after all, right at our fingertips.

The Bible warns us that the last generation of people on this earth before the coming of the Lord will be unique in many ways. If you look around, and maybe even look within, you can clearly see that what is described to us in 2 Timothy chapter 3 in relationship to the last generation seems to have arrived. Look closely at this description of those who will be wandering the planet just before Jesus comes for His people. 2 Timothy chapter 3 verses 1 through 5; *"This know also, that in the last days perilous times shall come. 2 For men shall be lovers of their own selves, covetous, boasters, proud, blasphemers, disobedient to parents, unthankful, unholy, 3 Without natural affection, trucebreakers, false accusers, incontinent, fierce, despisers of those that are good, 4 Traitors, heady, highminded, lovers of pleasures more than lovers of God; 5 Having a form of godliness, but denying the power thereof: from such turn away." (KJV)*

Mark(s) of the Beast

When I read this passage, I can't help but pause on the statement in verse 2 that in the last days there will be a generation that will be "lovers of their own selves." We are the generation after all, that invented something called the "selfie". All you must do is log on to any social media platform these days, and you will see a generation of people so consumed by themselves, and so consumed by maintaining a false impression of themselves, that truth seems to be a welcomed sacrifice.

Sin Creep

Not only that, but from these same internet media postings you will see a people overwhelmed with covetousness, boastful, proud, and blasphemous at their very core. I am not saying that we as Christians are guiltless either. In fact, I am not claiming myself to be free of any of this. It is a trap that any and all of us can fall into, even without really knowing it. Society today has mastered the art of "sin creep". What I mean by that is that there is so much taking up our time, and so much being poured into our minds from every direction, that many times we aren't even aware of how far we have drifted from the shoreline of grace and truth. We must check ourselves daily, or

Martin W Sondermann

maybe even by the hour, and sometimes by the very minute.

Blasphemy surrounds us all today. This generation (of all ages) have begun to discard something as real and profound as truth, and replaced it with "personal truth", which is no truth at all. What I mean by that is that moral relativity has taken over. Society now says that what is true for you is not true for me. This post-modern era holds to the philosophy that truth is only the concoction of the individual, and that any real truth is a collective understanding, but can change as needed.

To that understanding I ask the question; What about gravity?

You see there is truth in the Universe. All beings are affected by gravity. Gravity itself is a real force. It can be overcome by machines and technology, at least for a time. But, make no mistake gravity exists. But what if I decide I don't believe in gravity? What if I choose to believe my own truth that gravity doesn't exist? What if we all agree that it doesn't? Can I then walk off the Empire State Building and expect to float? Can I overcome gravity because I don't believe it to be true?

No, I cannot, and neither can you!

In the same way those who blaspheme God today and say that they have their own personal truth and that trumps God's truth. Or, even so-called Christians who claim that those things which are clearly sin, and detested by God, are somehow okay now. Can they deny the truth of God, and walk off the building expecting to float? Are all of those who deny the existence of Hell somehow immune from its eternal judgment?

No! They are not.

God's truth is absolute truth. There is no way around it no matter how much you fight, argue, or attempt to abolish it with your own opinion, or you very own sacred truth. The fact remains that there is nothing sacred about a lie, and as this world grows darker, many will embrace the darkness that denies the light.

We as Christians should be motivated by all of this. As we recognize the signs and times in which we live, we should dedicate ourselves to that Light. We should not get so discouraged that we give up, after all, Jesus told us these days would arrive. He also told us that this meant He was on His way!

Third, "Motivational Speakers"

The third reason I believe Christians should study topics relating to the last days, and even the tribulation is so that it might motivate us to preach the Gospel. For some, not much motivation is needed. However, for many, and I might even say most in the Church today, motivation to preach the Gospel to a lost and dying world is desperately needed.

Over 150,000 people die each day on planet earth. That's over 6,000 per hour, over 100 per minute, and about 2 people per second. Of those that pass we can be sure that on average around 66.6% of the people on the planet are dying without Christ. Even though I know the number is even more than that, there is about one-third, or 33.3% of the planet which claim to be Christian in various form. That leaves two-thirds which are not.

Now, if we wanted to be even more accurate, I think we can safely say that not all who claim to be Christians are in fact Christians. We know this from the Bible, and Jesus' own words in Matthew chapter 7 verses 21 through 23, *"Not everyone that saith unto me, Lord, Lord, shall enter into the kingdom of heaven; but he that doeth the will of my Father which is in heaven.22 Many will say to me in that day, Lord, Lord, have we not prophesied in thy name? and in thy name have cast out devils? and in thy name done many wonderful works? 23 And then will I profess unto them, I never knew you: depart from me, ye that work iniquity." (KJV)*

If half of those alive today who claim to be believers are believers in Jesus Christ that still leaves around 75% of the world's population that needs to hear the Gospel. I personally believe the number to be even higher than that, but even so, 75% of today's population of 7.5 billion is roughly 5.6 billion people.

What more motivation do we need?

I know that we as believers need all the motivation, we can get to preach the Gospel, and I believe that by studying topics like the mark of the beast and recognizing the times in which we live can motivate us to do so. If nothing else, it should encourage us to share with our family and friends.

Martin W Sondermann

None of us want any of them to have to endure the tribulation, and certainly none of us want them to spend an eternity separated from God and us in a real place called Hell.

Last, but Not Least

The last reason I believe that topics like this one are important is because of its placement in the Bible. We are studying a passage from Revelation chapter 13, but one of the best arguments for doing this can be found in chapter 1. I already discussed the outline of the book of Revelation found in chapter 1 verse 19. However, one thing I didn't point out then was the attached blessing found in verse 3. *"Blessed is he that readeth, and they that hear the words of this prophecy, and keep those things which are written therein: for the time is at hand." (KJV)*

God didn't want us to be afraid of the Book of Revelation. Some Christians I talk to are afraid to read it or say it's impossible to understand. But if that is true why would God attach a special blessing to this book?

I tell you; God is not a cruel Father. He is a loving Father, and He wants good things for His children. He attached a blessing to this book. If you and I will read it,

Mark(s) of the Beast

and hear it, and keep the things which are written in it, we will be blessed! What that blessing looks like is up to God, but any book in the Bible that states we will be blessed by reading, hearing, and keeping the things within its pages is something I want to study!

In my own experience as a Christian I can tell you that this book has blessed me tremendously. Not only will studying this book take you to nearly every other book of the Bible, not only will it open your eyes to the times in which we live, and not only will it make you wise about what is coming, it also gives you hope beyond hope. I have read the ending and we win!

We win because He wins!

Jesus Christ is coming again, and He has given us the knowledge of what will happen just before His victorious return, and even some of what is going to happen in the centuries following. Revelation explains to us that He is in complete and utter control, and that His plan, which was made before the world was made, will happen according to His great will and purpose!

Bonus Time

Martin W Sondermann

I have given you four reasons why I believe we should study topics like the one in this book, but I am sure there are several others. In fact, I want to give you a bonus reason why I believe this book is important to believers. It can help each one of us to be motivated to finish strong. The signs are all around us. Jesus Christ is coming for His bride. He will be here soon, and when He arrives don't you want to be one who finishes strong? I know I do.

I think by studying topics such as the one addressed in the pages of this book it can indeed help us to continue the fight. It can encourage us to see that the Lord is quickly approaching. Don't you want to make your Lord proud? I don't want to be one that is ashamed at His coming. There is a verse in the Bible that haunts me but motivates me at the same time. In 1 John chapter 2 verse 28 it says, *"And now, little children, abide in him; that, when he shall appear, we may have confidence, and not be ashamed before him at his coming." (KJV)*

I do not want to be one of His children that when He appears, I am not able to have confidence, but instead sink in shame. Not that I wouldn't be saved, but that I wouldn't finish the race well. I want to finish strong, and I hope you do as well.

Football Inserted, Because I Can!

I love the game of football. Over the years I have watched it, played it, coached it, and even written about it. There is such an amazing thing about the game of football. It has so many lessons that can be applied to life, and that means our spiritual life as well. If you know the game of football you know it is made up of four quarters, unless there is a need for overtime. Right now, I believe humanity finds itself in the fourth quarter, and we as the Church need to understand this. We have the ball, and there is only a short time left in the game. At this point it seems like we are behind on the scoreboard, but our destiny, and the destinies of others, depends on our final drive down that field. Will we choose to do all we can to secure victory, or will we crumble under the pressure? Will we sacrifice our blood, sweat, and tears to gain the prize, or will we give up in the face of a vicious opponent hitting us from every side?

In 2007 I was blessed enough to attend the Tostitos Fiesta Bowl. It was a game that featured a Goliath type football team from the University of Oklahoma versus a David like school called Boise State. In full disclosure my undergraduate degree is from Boise State, and I went to that game with high-hopes that the Broncos would find victory. Now, for you Oklahoma fans and non-Boise State fans, please forgive me. Don't stop reading just because of my alma mater. I am still your brother in the Lord.

In any case, there I was sitting in seat 7, row C, section 424-L. It was looking like a victory for my team until things started to unravel. Oklahoma tied the game up late, and then with just over a minute to go it looked like the Sooners sealed the game with a pick-6. For those who don't know football that just means Oklahoma intercepted a Boise State pass and ran it back for a touchdown. This gave the Sooners a 35-28 lead with 1:02 left in the game.

All seemed lost for the team from Boise. That is until with less than :20 left on the clock Boise State threw a pass that was caught by one Boise State receiver, but he tossed backward to another receiver running the other direction. It was a play called the "hook and lateral". The Boise State player now with the ball scored with just :07 seconds on the game clock. With the kicked extra point the game was then

158

tied at 35, and it went to overtime. Oklahoma scored quickly in OT, but Boise State answered on another trick play to come within one point.

At this point all of us in the stadium seemed exhausted and losing our voices. I can't imagine how tired every player on that field must have felt. It was a grueling contest. I remember just after the interception return by Oklahoma some local guys sitting near us got up, patted me on the shoulder, and said something to the affect that it was a great game, and wished us better luck next time. But me being the fan I am I answered back, "it ain't over yet." Those two men smiled, and one of them patted me again as if to comfort me, and then made their way out of the stadium. I often wonder what those two did when they found out it wasn't over, even if it looked like it was. They missed out on so much.

I wonder how many in the Church are just like the two men from Phoenix. They get up too early and leave without realizing there is much game left to be played. I wonder how many in the Church resign to the comfort of their own homes because they see no hope or no reason to continue. But the Lord wants us to keep going. He wants us to keep playing. He wants us to keep cheering, and to keep the hope we have within us alive.

With the score now 42-41 in favor of Oklahoma the Boise State coaching staff made an incredible decision. They weren't content with just tying the game up and facing another overtime. The coaches decided not to kick the extra point, but instead to attempt a two-point conversion. This would end the game either way. They called a play named "Statue Left", it was a modified version of a play called the "Statue of Liberty". As the quarterback, and almost every other Boise State player on the field directed the action to the right side of the field, an underhand behind-the-back hand off to the running back moving to the left sealed the victory. Boise State won 43-42 on a two-point conversion, and that game is still one of the most exciting in college football history.

Immediately following the action on the field, the same Boise State running back that had scored the game winning points was on the sideline being interviewed on national television. During that post-game conversation, he got down on one knee and asked his cheerleader girlfriend to

Mark(s) of the Beast

marry him right there for the world to see. She said yes! It was an incredible moment.

I was so blessed to be there, but not just because our team won. God also used that game in a big way to show me what was coming. As crazy as that sounds I am not kidding.

You see, you and I as believers we are in a game. It is tough game, and right now it seems like we might be losing. Some are leaving and going home to the comfort of their house patting some of us on the shoulder as they leave. Others remain and are hopeful even if they are exhausted. But here's what I know; victory is coming, and it ain't over yet!

Jesus Christ will be here soon for His Church. It is not a question of "if", but rather "when"? The answer is very soon!

Once He arrives, He is going to take His bride to be with Him forever. Much like that proposal on the sideline, and the joy that followed, multiply that by an infinite amount, and the joy you and I will experience as the Bridegroom comes for His Bride will be unspeakable. We

Martin W Sondermann

will then spend a glorious honeymoon with our Lord and be with Him forever!

I am sure that every coach, every player, and every Boise State fan in that stadium felt that the journey they had traveled was worth it. Some had a tougher journey than others, but each played their part. I am sure that the hard work the coaches and players put in day-in-and-day-out was worth it. I am sure the years of sacrifice were worth it. I am sure the money and time spent by the fans was worth it. When it was all said and done, and when the final score was sealed, anyone there that day rooting for the Broncos were not sorry they had made the journey. How much more will it be worth it for you and me if we finish strong the journey that God has given each one of us?

Hold on Church, Jesus is coming for His Bride! And, it will be worth it.

Chapter 12

The Tale of Two Kings

The King's Bride

History is advancing. Every second that goes by is another moment closer to the return of Jesus Christ. In the book of John chapter 14 verses 1-3 Jesus gave a promise that all believers can hold on to. *"Let not your heart be troubled: ye believe in God, believe also in me. 2 In my Father's house are many mansions: if it were not so, I would have told you. I go to prepare a place for you.3 And if I go and prepare a place for you, I will come again, and receive you unto myself; that where I am, there ye may be also." (KJV)*

This promise states that Jesus is coming for His Church, and in that promise, I believe is a beautiful picture of the rapture of the Church.

Because, we also know that Jesus will one day return to the earth and set up His Kingdom. He will rule the earth from Jerusalem for 1,000 literal years until a final judgment. This means the place He is preparing now isn't the Earth or the new Earth. The place He is preparing seems to be a temporary shelter for His Bride. You can argue with this timeline, and I won't be offended. But I believe the Scripture is very clear on this issue. We, as the Body of Christ, are going to be here on Earth ruling and reigning with Christ during the Millennium. However, what Jesus states in His promise in John 14 is that He is preparing a place for us so that He can, *"come again, and receive you unto myself; that where I am, there ye may be also."* This seems to indicate that He is coming to get us to take us to that place of preparation. This is not the same as coming back with Him to rule and reign on the Earth. No, this is something different.

In ancient Jewish wedding traditions, there is a beautiful order to things, and I believe it gives us insight into being a part of the Bride of Christ. While accounts vary slightly the basic steps most can agree upon.

In the early stages of the marriage there was a time of betrothal. This is when the bride and groom are set apart for marriage. This was usually done by the father choosing a bride for his son. This process involved a negotiated agreed upon price paid by the groom for the bride and establishing a marriage contract. This was a written contract (Ketubbah) in which the groom commits to supporting his future wife, and the bride indicates the value of her dowry. This was followed by a time of separation and cleansing, and an entering into the betrothal period known as the "Erusin". This was a period of time where the bride and groom were considered married to one another, but without consummation. Also, an official divorce would be needed for the breaking of the contract from this moment on. This divorce could only be initiated by the groom.

During the betrothal period there was a bit of mystery. The time-period of the betrothal was usually around a year, but even though the bride knew the approximate time, she didn't know the exact day or hour. The groom would surprise her by coming for her at a time determined by the groom's father. This was done when the father believed it was the proper timing, and when the son had completed what was known as a "Huppah". This was a canopy that was built for the bride and groom to stand under while completing the marriage ceremony, and a private place where the relationship could be consummated.

The wedding ceremony was completed with a blessing over wine, and it signaled the start of what was usually a seven-day party. For seven days the guests of the wedding celebrate, dance, and eat. It is a joyful occasion for all invited.

When you look at the basic parts of the Jewish wedding ceremony it is easy to see the comparison to our Lord and His Bride. You and I have been promised a Bridegroom. He has paid a price for you and me with His blood. He told us that He would return for us, but only after He goes to prepare a place for us. We also know that in Matthew chapter 24 verse 36 we read Jesus' own words regarding His return for His Bride; *"But of that day and hour knoweth no man, no, not the angels of heaven, but my Father only." (KJV)*

We know that Jesus will come for us the moment the Father says it's time. We also see the Jewish wedding tradition in the fact that Jesus will come at a time determined by the Father, and He will then take us to the place He has prepared for us. This will be the completion of the marriage, and it will be followed by a seven-year period of celebration.

Revelation 19 starting at verse 6; *"And I heard as it were the voice of a great multitude, and as the voice of many waters, and as the voice of mighty thunderings, saying, Alleluia: for the Lord God omnipotent reigneth. 7*

Mark(s) of the Beast

Let us be glad and rejoice, and give honour to him: for the marriage of the Lamb is come, and his wife hath made herself ready. 8 And to her was granted that she should be <u>arrayed in fine linen, clean and white</u>: for the fine linen is the righteousness of saints. 9 And he saith unto me, Write, Blessed are they which are called unto the marriage supper of the Lamb. And he saith unto me, These are the true sayings of God. 10 And I fell at his feet to worship him. And he said unto me, See thou do it not: I am thy fellowservant, and of thy brethren that have the testimony of Jesus: worship God: <u>for the testimony of Jesus is the spirit of prophecy</u>. 11 And I saw heaven opened, and behold a white horse; and he that sat upon him was called Faithful and True, and in righteousness he doth judge and make war. 12 His eyes were as a flame of fire, and on his head were many crowns; and he had a name written, that no man knew, but he himself. 13 And he was clothed with a vesture dipped in blood: and his name is called <u>The Word of God.</u> 14 And <u>the armies which were in heaven</u> followed him upon white horses, clothed <u>in fine linen, white and clean.</u> 15 And out of his mouth goeth a sharp sword, that with it he should smite the nations: and he shall rule them with a rod of iron: and he

Martin W Sondermann

treadeth the winepress of the fierceness and wrath of Almighty God. 16 And he hath on his vesture and on his thigh a name written, KING OF KINGS, AND LORD OF LORDS. (KJV)

Amen! What a passage of Scripture. First, we see the Wife, or Bride of Christ, clothed in clean white linen. They have been made clean by the blood of the Lamb. We also see that this Bride in verse 14 is in heaven with the Lord, and now they are going to return with Him to the earth.

That's you and I fellow Christians!

I also love that this passage speaks to the fact that the testimony of Jesus is the spirit of prophecy. I guess there is another reason to study the book of Revelation. But, beyond that I think it speaks to the sovereignty of God. The Holy Bible is the only book that so boldly predicts the future, and it always comes to pass the way it is written. It is the only book that can be measured in this way, and that's because God knows the beginning from the end. Also, when it speaks of the spirit of prophecy being the testimony of Jesus, we should all pay attention. This means that all true Biblical prophecy testifies of Him. He is the center.

Mark(s) of the Beast

Looking Back to Go Forward

When I started this study, I told you that as we went through all of this, and as we study it out, we should never forget the center of it all. That center is Jesus! Prophecy in the Bible speaks about Him, His people, and His plan.

Also, in verse 13 we see a breathtaking picture of our Lord with His garment dipped in blood. This speaks of His sacrifice which was all-sufficient to forgive us of our sins. In that same verse we see another name of our Lord, and that is The Word of God.

In John chapter 1 verse 1 we read; *"In the beginning was the Word, and the Word was with God, and the Word was God."* *(KJV)* Then in that same chapter verse 14 we see this; *"And the Word was made flesh, and dwelt among us, (and we beheld his glory, the glory as of the only begotten of the Father,) full of grace and truth."* *(KJV)*

May we never forget the fact that it was not just a Father sending His Son to die for us, but in the beautiful mystery of the Trinity we see that God Himself became flesh that He could save His children. The Word was with God, and the Word was God. Verses 2 through 4 explain further; *"The same was in the beginning with God. 3 All things were made by him; and without him was not any*

Martin W Sondermann

thing made that was made. 4 In him was life; and the life was the light of men." (KJV) Jesus is Lord. He is God. He is the one who created all things, and in Him was life and that life was the light of men. He gave us life, and through Him life exists.

There is No Comparison!

When you compare Jesus with the coming Anti-Christ you see a stark difference. In fact, to compare the two is absolute foolishness because there is no comparison. The Anti-Christ is a created man. Nothing more. Not only that, the power behind him, Satan, is also a created being. He is not as powerful as God in any way. He is not the opposite of God. He is a created being that decided to go his own way. He is no match for Jesus, and there is really no way to illustrate the difference between Jesus and Satan. In an effort to grasp even a pinch of the difference I would say it would be like a full-grown man with large feet equipped with large flat-soled boots fighting against an ant—with no feet at all. That ant has nowhere to run, and no ability to escape. And, yet, that example still isn't enough of a contrast between our Lord, and the devil, but you get the point.

Mark(s) of the Beast

The title of this chapter is "The Tale of Two Kings". However, it would be more accurately named "The Tale of The Only King and a Counterfeit". The Anti-Christ, the false-prophet, and Satan are a cheap knockoff. They are not the real deal, and their kingdom is for a moment in time allowed by an All-Powerful God who in His infinite wisdom has chosen this story to play out in such a way that His Kingdom will be glorified for time and eternity. We don't understand the mystery of it all right now, but someday each of us who have placed our trust in Jesus, first chosen by God, will understand that it was all for His great glory!

My Prayer

My prayer for every person reading this book is that no matter what you believe about the Mark of the Beast, the Rapture, the Tribulation, and future events, that you would allow this book to challenge, equip, and motivate you.

If you are already a follower of Yeshua (Jesus), then I pray the challenges and information presented within these pages will motivate you to study the Word of God like never before. I pray that what is presented in this book will get you thinking more about eternity, and the real fact that Jesus Christ will be here for His Church very soon. I hope

Martin W Sondermann

it provokes you to preach the Gospel, and to reach out to a world that so desperately needs the message of the Cross!

If you don't know Jesus yet, my hope is that this work brings you to a personal relationship with the King of Kings, and the Lord of Lords! I pray that every person with eyes or ears on this page will be "Marked by God". I pray that none of you will find yourselves in the midst of the great tribulation, but if you are, I pray you will not succumb to the marks of the beast.

The Gospel is a simple message. Mankind is fallen. From Adam, and the first sin in the Garden of Eden, mankind was lost. Every person born, is born with a sin nature, and has no way to enter eternity with the Lord. It is impossible in our sinful condition.

That's where Jesus comes in.

Yeshua, Jesus, our Lord and Savior, God in the Flesh, came to this world in the form of a small child. He lived a perfect sinless life, fulfilling the Law of God, and taking the punishment of our sins upon Himself. Isaiah 53:4-6 says, *"Surely he hath borne our griefs, and carried our sorrows: yet we did esteem him stricken, smitten of God, and afflicted. But he was wounded for our transgressions, he was bruised for our iniquities: the chastisement of our*

peace was upon him; and with his stripes we are healed.
All we like sheep have gone astray; we have turned every
one to his own way; and the LORD hath laid on him the
iniquity of us all." (KJV)

Yeshua took our sin on a Cross planted on the hill called Golgotha. He then proved His majesty by resurrecting the Third Day and ascended into Heaven with the promise that He would one day return for His people.

Are you one of His?
Do you want to be?

The Bible declares in Ephesians 2:8-9, *"For by grace are ye saved through faith; and that not of yourselves: it is the gift of God: Not of works, lest any man should boast."*

Simply receive the free gift right now.

Tribulation Saints

If you are reading this book from that time-period known as the tribulation, and you have not bowed in worship to the beast, I want you to know that there is hope. Jesus Christ is the same yesterday, today and forever! If you have placed your trust in Him, hold on! We will be there soon, but it will be our Lord leading the charge!

If you have not yet placed your trust in Jesus Christ, please here my words. Many people have claimed that "all roads lead to God". Well, that is true. All roads do lead to God. However, all roads do not lead to Heaven!

You see, every single one of you reading this book are going to stand in front of God Almighty very soon. The Bible tells us that eternal judgment in Hell will come to those that have not placed their faith in Jesus Christ. God will judge you for your sin if you are not covered with the atoning blood of Jesus Christ. If you are not born again the Death Angel will not pass you over.

The bottom line is this; while all roads lead to God, there is only ONE ROAD that leads to Heaven! There is only ONE ROAD to eternal life with God in His Kingdom. The name of that road is the Highway of Holiness, Jesus Christ, Yeshua Hamashiach!

It's not too late for you if you haven't received the mark of the beast, whatever that mark, or marks, may be. It's not

Mark(s) of the Beast

too late for you if you haven't bent your knee in worship to the false god of this world.

Jesus (Yeshua) said that He is The Way, The Truth, and The Life. He said that no man comes to the Father, except through Him. Yes, there are many doors to judgment, but only ONE DOOR that leads to eternal life with God Almighty! Give your life over to Him, and trust in Him. Believe His Word and seek it for within the pages of the Bible where you will find peace even in a world without it.

Look to the Bible for the One that has all truth. He is known by many names, but He is the Only God! Hold on to the truth, as I have previously mentioned, we will be there soon. Look to the sky because the one leading us is like no other. His name is Jesus, but He is also known as; **The Advocate, The Almighty, The Lord of Lords, The King of Kings, The Amen, Counselor, Creator, The Door, The Way, The Truth, The Life, Everlasting Father, Prince of Peace, The Faithful Witness, The Branch, The Alpha and the Omega, The Arm of the Lord, The Word of God, the True Vine, Shiloh, The Shepard of our Souls, The Rock, The Root of David, Redeemer, The Judge of Israel, The King of Saints, The Lawgiver, The Lord of Glory, The Man of Sorrows, Jehovah, Emmanuel, Martin W Sondermann**

Deliverer, Desire of the Nations, Elect of God, The Horn of Salvation, The Holy One of Israel, Head of the Church, Heir of All Things, The First Begotten, The Chief Shepard, Christ, The First and Last, Great High Priest, The Lamb, Redeemer, The Seed of the Woman, The Resurrection and the Life, The Rose of Sharon, The Lilly of the Valley, The King of the Jews, The King of the Ages, Son of David, Son of the Highest, The Lamb, Messiah, The I AM, Jesus of Nazareth, and the Author and the Finisher of our Faith.

The End....

....is near

Look up! For your redemption draws near!

Mark(s) of the Beast

i   Dickens, Charles, A Tale of Two Cities, 1859 In the Public Domain

ii   New American Standard Bible. La Habra, CA: Lockman Foundation 1977

iii   King James Bible. 1769 In the Public Domain

iv   The Merriam Webster Dictionary. 1828. 1864

v   Strong's Concordance. 1890

vi   Cellan-Jones, R. (2014, Dec. 2). Stephen Hawking warns artificial intelligence could end mankind. Retrieved-from https://www.bbc.com/news/technology-30290540

vii   Kharpal, A. (2017, February 13). Elon Musk: Humans must merge with machines-or-become-irrelevant-in-AI-age.-Retrieved-from https://www.cnbc.com/2017/02/13/elon-musk-humans-merge-machines-cyborg-artificial-intelligence-robots.html

viii   Rose, G. (n.d.). Geordie Rose – Quantum Computing: Artificial Intelligence-is-Here.-Lecture-presented-on-YouTube-as-Video.https://www.youtube.com/watch?v=PqN_2jDVbOU

ix   George-J.-Laurer-(n.d.).Retrieved-from http://en.wikipedia.org/wiki/George_J._Laurer

x   Stockman,-H.-(1948).-Communication-by-Means-of-Reflected-Power.*ProceedingsoftheIRE,36*(10),1196-1204. doi:10.1109/jrproc.1948.226245

xi   Cryptocurrency.(n.d.).Retrieved-from https://en.oxforddictionaries.com/definition/cryptocurrency

Martin W Sondermann

Made in the USA
Monee, IL
05 April 2021